THE LIVING TRUST ALTERNATIVE

HOW A LIVING TRUST CAN HELP YOU TO AVOID PROBATE, SAVE TAXES, AND MORE

Expanded Second Edition

LOUIS AUSTIN
Living Trust Attorney

Published by Hudspeth Publishing Company, Kansas City, MO

DEDICATED TO:

Louis E. Schumacher, Sr., & "Topper" Schumacher
Carl L. Schumacher, Sr., & Gertrude Schumacher
Ludwig Schumacher & Elizabeth Schumacher
James A. Price & Johnnie G. Price
John T. Griffin & Mittie V. Griffin
Dora G. Lockhart
Willie Mae Lockhart
Robert G. Price
J.B.D.

"In good hands, a living trust is a dream machine."

PLEASE READ THIS: The information contained in The Living Trust Alternative is intended to provide accurate and authoritative information about the subject matter covered. But please be aware that laws and procedures change constantly and are subject to different interpretations. This book is sold with the understanding that the publisher and the author are not engaged in rendering legal, accounting or other professional services. If legal advice or other expert assistance is required, you should employ the services of a competent professional. The ultimate responsibility for making good decisions is yours.

Published by Hudspeth Publishing Company

First Edition published March 1988 as A Will Is Not The Way -
The Living Trust Alternative and Avoid Probate-The Living Trust Alternative.
Second Printing, April 1989
Third Printing, April 1990
Fourth Printing, September 1990
Second Edition Published, July 1995

This publication is available for bulk purchase. For information:
Hudspeth Publishing Company
5904 East Bannister Road
Kansas City, Missouri 64134-1141
(816)765-3900

ISBN: 0-9625528-3-6
Library of Congress Catalog Card Number 94-096467

Printed in the United States of America

TABLE OF CONTENTS

TABLE OF CONTENTS

Have you made any plans to distribute your property and take care of your family when you die or if you become incompetent? If you have, you probably used a will, joint ownership, power of attorney, or a transfer on death designation. Maybe you haven't done anything at all—that's not unusual. Any of these traditional estate planning methods (and doing nothing is *very* traditional) can work—because even if you haven't written a will, the state you live in has written one for you. But all of these methods have risks associated with them and will lead to probate sooner or later.

Regrettably, most people don't realize what this can mean until it is too late. That's why we wrote this book. We want you to know about the risks, especially what can happen to you, your family and your property during probate. For example, did you know:

Δ   A will does not avoid probate

Δ   Probate costs average 5% to 10% of your estate's *gross* value

Δ   The probate process usually takes at least a year—and often even longer

Δ   Probate files are public record and anyone can have access to your file

Δ   Your will can easily be contested

Δ   The probate court can take control of you and your property before you die

Δ   You may not be able to sell jointly owned property without approval from the probate court

Δ   The probate court—not your child's guardian—will probably control your child's inheritance

Also, you may not know that you have another traditional estate planning alternative—a living trust.

A living trust avoids all probate and lets you keep complete control, even if you become incapacitated or incompetent. With a living trust, you will have the security of knowing that your plan will *stay* your plan—it won't be altered by the court, greedy relatives or unforeseen legal technicalities.

THERE ARE A FEW THINGS ABOUT THIS BOOK WE'D LIKE YOU TO KNOW.

First, we wrote this book for you, the public, *not* for attorneys. We have written it in clear, conversational English and have intentionally avoided the use of technical legal terms wherever possible.

Second, we are presenting this information as a general overview. In order to keep it as understandable as possible, we haven't gotten bogged down with specific laws and regulations, complicated tax discussions or every conceivable situation that could come up. You may find some minor variations in your state's laws, but generally these will be technical and won't affect the overall message. (For example: some states require a guardian to post a bond and some don't; some states use the term *executor* while some use *personal representative*; etc.)

Third—and this is *very* important—this book is *not* a "do-it-yourself" manual. There are more and more do-it-yourself estate planning books springing up all the time, especially mail order will and living trust kits. Most of these are quick to condemn the entire legal profession, and this "hype" does sell a lot of books. There's no question that some attorneys do deserve it. We agree that the legal profession could and should do a better job of educating and informing the public about all of its estate planning choices. But we don't think the solution is to condemn an entire profession and try to do this yourself. In fact, that can be very dangerous. Some of these do-it-yourself plans contain misleading, even incorrect, information. And because they are generic in content, they cannot begin to address every family's unique needs (not to mention the differences in state laws).

If you rely on a do-it-yourself package for guidance, you should know your risks—you could unknowingly be creating some real problems later on. Remember, we're talking about *your family.* Risking their future is simply not worth it. In short—*don't do it yourself.*

We do believe you need an attorney to advise you and prepare the legal documents for you, but you need the *right* attorney. We have devoted an entire section in this book to helping you find an attorney who is experienced in preparing living trusts and can do yours at a reasonable cost. We have also included an Information Form that will help you get your relevant personal information organized. You will probably still have some questions to ask your attorney about your own individual situation, but you'll be better educated and organized after reading this book—and that will save you time and money.

In summary, we think it's a tragedy that so many families continue to suffer through probate just because they're not informed. They don't understand how probate works or that they can completely avoid probate with a living trust. Ideally, everyone should have a living trust. The first step, though, is understanding living trusts. To do so, you need information that is accurate and easy to comprehend. That's the purpose of this book—to provide you with enough good information that you can make informed decisions about what's best for you and your family— before it's too late!

We sincerely hope the information in this book benefits you and your family.

Yours very truly,

Cindy Sue Davis   **Louis Austin**

Louis Austin was born and raised in the Midwest. After graduating from the University of Missouri-Kansas City School of Law in 1974, he spent seven years as General Counsel for a commercial real estate developer who specialized in the conversion of underground limestone mines into warehouse/office space. As legal counsel during this unique and innovative development, Mr. Austin gained extensive experience in every aspect of real estate law. Titling requirements, which are essential to every properly prepared living trust estate plan, were especially important.

After entering private practice in 1981, Mr. Austin investigated living trusts when a 94-year-old client was declared incompetent. The assets belonging to this client had all been placed into a conservatorship and dealing with the probate system was frustrating and cumbersome for the family. Satisfied that the living trust alternative offered families the advantage of handling their affairs privately during times of incapacity and death, without the need for probate court involvement, Mr. Austin decided to change his firm's practice exclusively to living trust estate planning. The firm changed its name to Austin Living Trust to establish itself as a dedicated living trust practice. Austin Living Trust became one of the first law firms in the United States to promote and market the revocable living trust as an alternative to the financial and emotional costs of probate.

Mr. Austin extensively researched the history of revocable living trusts under the guidance of the late William F. Fratcher, formerly the Faculty Emeritus at the University of Missouri-Columbia School of Law. In 1988, Mr. Austin responded to the public's many questions and authored *The Living Trust Alternative*, which has sold over 200,000 copies and is now in its expanded second edition.

Known to many as the "voice of living trust," Mr. Austin conducts workshops and seminars throughout the United States to educate the public about the advantages of the living trust. He frequently guest lectures at living trust workshops for government agencies, foundations, civic and religious organizations. His many media appearances include the Business Radio Network and CNBC's "Smart Money With The Dolans." Mr. Austin lives in Kansas City, Missouri and is a member of the Missouri Bar Association.

The law firm of Austin Living Trust is head-quartered in Kansas City, Missouri. Preparing and servicing living trust estate plans is Austin's only business. The firm has created thousands of living trust estate plans and, through its Kansas City office, currently prepares trust documents for residents of Missouri, Kansas and nineteen other states. Every Austin living trust is individually customized for each client's situation and estate planning needs.

Unlike most law firms, Austin's pricing is based on flat rates which include customization and all supporting documents. This law firm believes that clients should be self-sufficient to minimize their expense and maintain their privacy. That is why the firm teaches its clients how to put assets directly into their own living trust. Austin provides the necessary transfer letters and instructions. All Austin trust clients are entitled to unlimited phone and office consultations. This service, provided at no charge, ensures that the client can always get questions answered and that all of the client's property is correctly titled in the trust name. All Austin clients work directly with an attorney, who conducts client interviews, answers questions, drafts and approves legal documents, supervises trust signings and services clients.

The firm does not use any "generic" materials or software. Instead, Austin researches, develops and copyrights all of its trust documents, software and educational materials. These materials are used exclusively by Austin Living Trust clients so that the firm can maintain its high standard of quality control. Austin trust documents are subjected to rigid internal quality control specifications and continuously reviewed, upgraded and improved. In addition, the firm's documents are periodically examined by nationally recognized outside legal counsel.

As an independent law firm, Austin is not affiliated with any banking, insurance or financial institution. The firm conducts free workshops throughout the metropolitan Kansas City area to educate the public about the living trust alternative to probate. In keeping with the firm's philosophy of autonomy, all workshops are sponsored by Austin and conducted by an Austin Living Trust attorney. Participation by outside organizations and speakers is not permitted. Austin Living Trust is nationally recognized as one of the leaders in the living trust field.

Our goal is to protect America's families from probate

CONTRIBUTING EDITORS

We wish to acknowledge the following individuals who acted as technical advisors and reviewers for this book:

Cindy Sue Davis is the General Manager of Austin Living Trust. She has been with the firm since 1982 and previously worked for a California mortgage company and a Kansas City commercial real estate company. She acts as liaison between the attorneys and internal operations to ensure the efficient processing of trust documents in conformity with Austin's quality control standards. Mrs. Davis is responsible for the development, maintenance and safeguarding of Austin's copyrighted computer data base. She supervises all of the firm's daily activities such as client and workshop scheduling, media placement and speaking appearances, quality control checks, purchasing, and monitoring client file status. Mrs. Davis works directly with Louis Austin in developing the firm's marketing programs and implementing revisions to its trust documents. Her twelve years of experience and familiarity with every facet of a living trust law firm, especially client servicing, make her uniquely qualified to serve as a contributing editor of this book.

Jennifer L. Finch has been an attorney with Austin Living Trust since 1988. She practices exclusively in the area of living trusts. In addition to working directly with clients to help them set up their living trust estate plans, she conducts weekly living trust workshops sponsored by Austin Living Trust. She has also been a speaker for many community organizations, including the Volunteer Attorney Project with the office of Legal Aid of Western Missouri. Mrs. Finch graduated from the University of Missouri-Kansas City School of Law where she was recognized for outstanding service to the Phi Alpha Delta Law Fraternity. She is licensed by both Kansas and Missouri and is a member of the Missouri Bar Association.

William F. Fratcher contributed as the technical advisor on the history of the living trust. An internationally recognized expert on trust law, he served as Faculty Emeritus for the University of Missouri-Columbia School of Law. He was General Reporter on Trust Law for the International Encyclopedia of Comparative Law (1966-1974). At the time of his death, he was finalizing the Fourth Edition of *Scott on Trusts* in twelve volumes. Professor Fratcher's generous assistance in researching the history of the living trust is deeply appreciated. He was a true scholar in every sense of the word and dedicated to the highest standards of legal and historical accuracy. His suggestions, critiques and support were instrumental in writing this expanded second edition of *The Living Trust Alternative.*

John G. Dyer is Legal Counsel for the Babson Mutual Fund Group head-quartered in Kansas City, Missouri. He is President of the Missouri Mutual Funds Association, Vice-President and Legal Counsel of the UMB Mutual Fund Group, and former Director of the Kansas City Economic Development Corporation. He is featured in *Who's Who in American Law* and is designated as a Certified Employee Benefit Specialist.

David E. Price is a partner in the Evansville, Indiana law firm of Price, Bradley & Collins. Following his graduation from law school, Mr. Price was employed by the U.S. Department of Treasury, Internal Revenue Service, in Richmond, Virginia and Indianapolis, Indiana as senior trial attorney. Mr. Price frequently speaks on the topics of "Estate Planning with Living Trusts" and "Business Succession Planning" throughout the United States at seminars and corporate meetings. He is special estate planning counsel to Franklin Life Insurance Company of Springfield, Illinois and a member of the Indiana, Kentucky and Cincinnati Bar Associations.

8 GOOD PLANS CAN GO WRONG

Mary was a widow with no children or immediate family. In her will she left everything in equal shares to three institutions which had each been an important part of her life: to her husband's university for scholarships in his memory; to her neighborhood church; and to a children's hospital, where her only child had been treated for a terminal illness many years ago.

When Mary died, her will had to be probated before her property could be given to these institutions. As required by law, a notice of her death was published in the newspaper, and a list of all of her assets was made public. Some distant relatives (who Mary barely knew) saw the notice in the paper, hired an attorney and filed a lawsuit. They claimed Mary was incompetent when she signed her will, so it was not valid. The institutions had to hire attorneys to try to uphold Mary's will, and Mary's estate also had to be represented by an attorney. A nasty and expensive legal battle began. Finally, more than four years later, the institutions agreed to give Mary's relatives half of her estate, just to end the fight. This was obviously not what Mary had wanted.

Betty, recently divorced, had a 3-year-old daughter named Lauren. Betty had heard that she should have a will (especially since she had a child). When she saw an advertisement for a will kit, she ordered one through the mail. In her will, she left everything to Lauren. She didn't have that much property, so she increased her life insurance and listed Lauren as beneficiary. She named her sister, Linda, as Lauren's guardian, thinking Linda would be able to use the life insurance money to raise Lauren if Betty could not.

When Betty was killed in a car accident a few years later, her will went through probate. Because Lauren was a minor, the court had to establish a probate guardianship for her. The court did allow Linda to be Lauren's guardian, but the court kept control of the inheritance, including everything Betty left Lauren in her will *and* the money from the life insurance company (which would not pay direct to Lauren because she was under age). When Lauren turned 18, the legal age in that state, she received all of her inheritance in one lump sum. She (and her boyfriend) quickly spent it in one year of extravagant living.

Betty's will kit did not inform her that the court, not the guardian, would have control of the inheritance; that insurance companies will not pay death benefits directly to a minor child; or that a minor receives the full inheritance when he/she reaches legal age.

Dorothy, a widow, put all of her property, including her house, into joint ownership with her married son. She did this because she thought that when she died, her property would automatically go to her son without the need for probate. Several years later, her son and his wife separated, and Dorothy decided to sell her house so she could move in with her son. But she soon discovered she could not sell it without her *daughter-in-law's* signature on the deed. The daughter-in-law was still legally married to her son and was entitled by law to a "marital interest" in the property. The title company would not insure clear title to the buyer without the daughter-in-law's signature because it wasn't clear what her "interest" would be—and she refused to sign unless she would get part of the money when the house was sold. Dorothy was stuck. She didn't know that joint ownership with a married person includes *that person's spouse*. And because Dorothy had placed her house in joint ownership, she lost control of her own home.

On the advice of a neighbor, Frank and Elizabeth, an elderly couple, put everything they owned, including their home and stocks, in their unmarried adult daughter's name. They believed that this would avoid probate (and the Medicaid "spend down" provisions if they had to go to a nursing home) and that all their property would pass directly to their daughter—their only child—when they were both gone. A year later, Frank died of a heart attack. Several months after that, their daughter was suddenly killed in an auto accident.

Elizabeth never imagined that she would survive both her husband and daughter. To add to her distress, Elizabeth now owned nothing in her own name—everything was in her deceased daughter's name. She was forced to probate her daughter's estate to get back her own property. During this long process she had to rely on the court to grant her living expenses. Sometimes the court would approve them, sometimes not. And during a declining stock market, she helplessly watched the value of her stocks fall to only a fraction of their previous value because the court could not react in time for them to be sold quickly. Elizabeth lost her financial independence plus a substantial portion of her assets to probate. And she was just trying to get back what belonged to her in the first place.

John and Ellen had each been married before and had small children from their first marriages. When they married, they considered it a fresh start and one family. They put all of their property in both their names (joint ownership) with the intention that, when they died, all the children would receive an equal share. They didn't make a will because they thought joint ownership would serve the same purpose.

A living trust would have prevented these unexpected problems

When John died everything went to Ellen, and she continued to raise and care for all the children. When Ellen died many years later, her property had to go through probate. Under the probate laws of that state, Ellen's property could only be distributed to *her surviving blood children*. Since John's children were not of Ellen's blood and had never been legally adopted by Ellen, they received nothing. Even though John and Ellen considered all of the children as their own, equally, the probate laws did not. Because they relied on joint ownership, they unknowingly disinherited John's children.

When Edward and Beth married, they both had children and property from previous marriages. They had new wills drawn up and each left the property they had acquired before their marriage to their own children. Edward died ten years later. His will left title to his 600-acre family farm to his two sons, who were farming it.

While Edward's will was in probate, Beth's attorney advised her that as a surviving spouse in the state in which she lived, she was entitled to a percentage of all of Edward's property, including the farm. Although Beth knew that Edward had wanted the farm to go solely to his sons, she felt that she and her children had a right to part of it and decided to contest Edward's will. This prompted a bitter court battle, with Beth and her children on one side, and Edward's sons on the other. Eventually, Beth won and was granted a percentage of the farm, but the family closeness established during Edward's lifetime was destroyed. Edward's will offered no protection to his children and did not guarantee that his wishes would be carried out.

Rosalind, an elderly widow, named her three adult children as "transfer on death beneficiaries" on all of her property including her home. She thought this would avoid probate and guarantee that each of her children would receive an equal share at her death.

Shortly afterwards, Rosalind had a massive stroke which left her incompetent. Her children soon discovered that they had no authority as beneficiaries to manage their mother's affairs because Rosalind was still the owner of her property. They had to hire a lawyer to have the court declare Rosalind incompetent and set up a probate conservatorship so they could manage her affairs. This also meant that the court had to approve every decision about Rosalind's care and finances, which was very time-consuming, complicated and expensive. The court, not Rosalind's children, was in control. Rosalind's family found out the hard way that transfer on death designations do not avoid probate.

A living trust would easily have prevented all of these unexpected problems and many others like them!

Y ou can't appreciate the advantages of a living trust until you understand what can happen to you and your family in probate.

Nearly everyone has heard of probate, but most people really don't know what it means—until they experience it. In this section, we will tell you the truth about probate so you can avoid it by setting up a living trust—before it's too late to do anything.

What Is Probate?

Probate is the legal process through which, when you die, your bills are paid and your assets are distributed based upon what your will says (if you have one) or what the law says (if you don't). Probate also takes control for those who cannot handle their own affairs because they are incompetent or are minor children. The court will control both their finances and personal affairs while they are not able to take care of themselves—until the incompetent person recovers or dies, or until the minor child legally becomes an adult.

Probate is the only way to legally transfer title to any titled property (such as real estate, cars, bank accounts, stocks and bonds, etc.) when the person listed as the owner cannot sign his/her name due to death, incompetence or because he/she is a minor.

Why Does Probate Exist?

Probate has existed in one form or another for hundreds of years. It was created with the best of intentions to protect you, your property and your family. It provided an orderly method of paying bills and transferring ownership of property at death, and for managing the financial affairs of an incompetent person or minor child—all under the direct supervision of the court system.

So, What's Wrong With Probate?

The probate process is simply obsolete. Probate was, and still is, a very slow and cumbersome process. It is a product of the "horse and buggy days," when it took months to locate and notify relatives and creditors of a death or illness. Back then it didn't matter that probate took a long time, but today it does. Things move much more quickly today. We can communicate with friends and relatives anywhere in the world in just seconds, and many times financial decisions must be made within hours. Times have changed, but probate has not. In California, for example, the

The

probate

process

is

obsolete

average probate takes two years, and some cases go on for five years and longer.

Besides taking a long time, probate is expensive and inflexible. Once the process begins, you and your family lose control and the court takes over. Probate is a complicated legal process. It can only go by exactly what the law tells it to do, and only when the law says to do it. Probate, with its rigid requirements, costs and painstakingly slow process, can cause all kinds of unexpected problems for today's families.

When Probate Can Get You

Very simply, unless you take the proper action now, probate can and probably will affect you and your family in at least one of the following three ways:

Δ   When you die

Δ   If you become incompetent

Δ   If your minor children inherit property

There are only two sure ways to avoid probate: Own nothing in your own name, not even a bank account. Realistically, how many of us could live like that? Or you can get a living trust.

Here in Part One, we'll look at how you and your family can end up under the control of the probate court in each of these three situations, and what happens if you do. But first, let's look at some traditional methods people use to try to avoid probate, and why in many cases these methods don't work the way people think they will.

COMMON MYTHS ABOUT AVOIDING PROBATE

Myth 1: "I have a will, so my family won't have to go through probate when I die."

False! Having a will does *not* avoid probate. A will can have no effect unless it goes through the probate process and, in fact, *must* be admitted to the probate court to be legal and enforceable. Your will must be validated as being authentic before ownership of your assets can be transferred to your heirs, and the probate court is the only way this can be done—that's its job. So, in effect, a will is a one-way ticket to probate.

A handwritten will (called a "holographic will") doesn't avoid probate either. It's still a will. And it may create other problems because many states will not accept a handwritten will.

Many people believe that if they have a will with a trust in it, the trust lets them avoid probate. But, as we just explained, *all* wills—including those with trusts in them—must go through probate. The trust cannot go into effect until *after* the will has been probated.

Myth 2: "I don't have a will, so there will be no need for my family to go through probate when I die."

False, again! Even if *you* haven't written a will (after all, the law gives you the option of "doing nothing"), *the state has written one for you.* Every state has laws for the distribution of property for those who die without a will. So if you don't have a will when you die, the state has to make sure your debts are paid and your property is distributed *according to the laws of that state*—which may or may not be the way you would have wanted. Consider, for example, the true story of the famous movie actor, James Dean:

His mother died when he was a small child, and his father sent him to live with an aunt and uncle who raised him. James, who had grown very close to his "new" family, had talked about wanting his aunt and uncle to receive most of his property if something happened to him, and particularly had expressed a desire to provide for his young cousin's college education. But he never got around to making out a will. When he was killed suddenly in a car accident, his estate went through probate. Since he did not have a will, his property was distributed according to California law (the state's will). Everything he owned was given to his father, who was his closest surviving relative, even though there was practically no contact between them through the years. Under the terms of the state's will, his aunt and uncle (who had devoted years of their lives to raising and loving him) and his cousin were given nothing. Do you think this is what James Dean would have wanted to happen?

Myth 3: "I own everything jointly, so when I die all my property will immediately go to the other owner without probate."

Maybe, but look out! Joint ownership is a way of titling property, not an estate plan. It does not *guarantee* that you will avoid probate and can create all kinds of unexpected problems.

A will is a one-way ticket to probate

The kind of joint ownership that most people have is called "joint tenancy with right of survivorship." This means that when one of the owners dies, his/her share instantly becomes the property of the surviving joint owner. It is often used by husbands and wives or between parents and their adult children in an effort to avoid probate—and in many situations it does work. For instance, if both your name and your spouse's name is on the titles of all the property you own, ownership will immediately transfer to the surviving spouse when one of you dies, without probate.

Unanticipated Problems

But joint ownership can throw you some unexpected curves. If, for example, both you and your spouse are in an accident and die at the same time, your jointly-owned property will *have* to be probated before it can go to your heirs, whether you had a will or not. Or, let's say you successfully use joint ownership to avoid probate and your share transfers to your surviving spouse when you die, but for some reason your spouse does not add another joint owner. When your spouse dies, then the entire estate (your spouse's estate plus what you left your spouse) must go through probate before ownership can be transferred to the rest of your heirs. So you didn't avoid probate after all—you just postponed it.

Loss of Control

When most people think of joint ownership, they immediately think of a joint banking account between husband and wife. But a joint banking account is not the same as joint ownership of property (real estate, stocks, bonds, etc.). A joint bank account is actually a contract with the bank that allows each joint "owner" to independently make deposits, withdrawals, or even close the account. Joint ownership o*f property* is something altogether different. To transact any business (buy, sell, get a loan, refinance, etc.) requires the signature of all the owners. For real estate, the signature of every owner's spouse is also required. *One owner cannot act independently*, so you can easily lose control, especially if the other owner can't or won't sign. It's easy to see how people get confused. Just remember you do *not* have the same flexibility and control with joint ownership of property as you do with a joint banking account.

Unintentionally Disinheriting Your Children

Blind reliance on joint ownership can cause you to unintentionally disinherit your own children. Consider this disaster:

Marie, an elderly widow, had a will which left everything in equal shares to her five grown children. When she learned she had cancer, she put everything she owned into joint ownership with her oldest son, thinking this would avoid probate and make things easier for her family when she died. She discussed it with her son and was sure that he would carry out her wishes and divide everything equally among the children. When she died, ownership did immediately go to her son, but he died suddenly in a construction accident a few weeks later, *before* the property could be distributed. His wife, only recently married to Marie's son, claimed everything as his surviving spouse, and she decided to keep it all herself! Marie's will (which, remember, left everything in equal shares to her children) was powerless, because as soon as she died *she no longer owned anything*. Immediately upon her death all ownership transferred to her son, so *there was nothing left to will*. Marie's joint ownership plan did avoid probate, but it also disinherited her children!

Remarriage and joint ownership can cause some very undesirable results. For instance, you remarry and add your new spouse as joint owner on all your property. You have children from a previous marriage. If you die first, your spouse automatically owns the entire property (including your share). When your spouse dies, the property will go to your spouse's heirs—and since *your children* are not heirs of your spouse (unless your spouse has legally adopted them), your children are disinherited.

Even if your spouse includes your children in his/her current will, you still can't be sure they will inherit. Your spouse could always write a new will disinheriting your children. He/she could also add another joint owner (such as a new spouse) who would then receive full ownership of the property when your spouse dies.

You lose control when you make someone else a joint owner of your property, and you have no way of controlling who will ultimately receive your share of the property.

Incompetency

You can really end up in a mess if one of the joint owners becomes incapacitated or incompetent and can no longer sign his/her name—especially if real estate is involved. The other owner will have to get approval from the probate court before any jointly owned property can be sold. This is because *both* signatures are required to transfer title and if one of the co-owners cannot sign his/her name, *only the court* can sign for that owner. So, in effect, the court becomes a joint owner. And once the court gets involved, it stays involved until that person recovers or dies. This whole issue of incapacity and incompetency—and the involvement of the probate court—is so important (and something that so few people know about) that we've included an entire section on it, beginning on *Page 32.*

Lawsuits

You could also end up in a lawsuit. If you are a joint owner with someone who is sued over an incident which involves the jointly owned piece of property, you will quite likely be named in the lawsuit, even if you have done nothing. Think about this example:

Robert and Toni wanted to help their 18-year-old son get a car, so they co-signed the loan and listed themselves as co-owners with their son on the title. Shortly thereafter, the son was at fault in an accident in which the other driver was seriously injured. When the injured person filed suit for personal injury. Robert and Toni were sued along with their son. Their personal assets are now at risk—they could be frozen, even seized, to help settle the claim.

Don't become a co-owner. Just think for a moment about how "lawsuit-happy" our society is these days. Joint ownership can leave you wide open for a possible lawsuit.

Bankruptcy

Joint ownership exposes your property to the co-owner's creditors. If a joint owner files bankruptcy, he/she must file a list of all jointly owned property (checking and savings accounts, stocks, bonds, real estate, etc.) with the court. This means that the bankruptcy court will now have control of your property. The court could order the sale of your property to pay the other joint owner's creditors. *Before* you add a joint owner on your property ask yourself "is this worth the risk of exposing my property to someone else's creditors?"

Tenancy-ln-Common

There is another kind of joint ownership, used less frequently, called "tenancy-in-common." Even though it works very differently from "joint tenancy with right of survivorship," people often confuse them. Under tenancy-in-common, when one of the owners dies, that owner's share will go to his/her heirs—*not to the other co-owner*. If you own property with someone through a tenancy-in-common arrangement, you could find

With joint ownership you're playing "Russian roulette" with your family.

yourself with several new co-owners when that person dies and the heirs receive the property. Sometimes it's hard enough to get two people to agree. Imagine how difficult it could be to get several owners to reach an agreement, especially if you are trying to sell real estate. You could also have the same problems we mentioned earlier (incompetence, lawsuits, etc.) and, with *several* owners involved, your risks are even greater.

To avoid confusion, when we refer to joint ownership in this book we are referring to the more common "joint tenancy with right of survivorship."

Joint Ownership—The Bottom Line

Joint ownership may work for you—if *everything* goes exactly the way you hope. But then again, maybe it won't. With joint ownership you're playing "Russian roulette" with your family. You can still end up in probate, especially if a joint owner becomes incapacitated or incompetent. Furthermore, you can unintentionally disinherit your own children and expose your property to the lawsuits and bankruptcies of the other joint owners. Is it worth the risks?

Myth 4: "I have a power of attorney, so I don't need a will or joint ownership to avoid probate."

False! Some people give power of attorney (often called a "general" power of attorney) to a spouse or adult child, assuming it will allow titles to their property to be transferred without probate when they die or become incompetent. Actually, a power of attorney is automatically revoked at death or incompetency, so it won't be of any use then. Some states permit a "durable" power of attorney which remains valid if you become incompetent, but it, too, is automatically revoked at death. Remember, that all powers of attorney are revoked when the signer dies.

If you think a durable power of attorney will protect you if you become incompetent, think again. Armed with a durable power of attorney, it would be very easy for someone to "raid your estate" if you are incompetent. This person would be able to transfer titles to your property and accounts to his or her name, and in your condition you probably wouldn't even know about it. You could recover from your incompetency, only to find you have no property or accounts because all of the titles have been changed! You may have a hard time getting your property back. You'll probably have to file a lawsuit, and by the time it's settled there may not be anything left.

Anyone can reject your power of attorney

In many situations a power of attorney doesn't work at all. Since it is not a contract, anyone can refuse to accept it. Some companies will not accept a power of attorney unless it is on their own form. Banks and brokerage companies routinely reject powers of attorney. Instead, they require an order from a probate court because this order protects them from liability. You should know that the older the power of attorney is, the less likely that it will be accepted. Banks, brokerage houses, title companies, etc., are suspicious of old powers of attorney and often reject them outright, even in routine transactions. It can also be very difficult to use a power of attorney for property located in another state, due to the differences in state laws. Finally, with a power of attorney, you are permitting someone else the right to sign your name for you while you are still alive, with total freedom to do with your property as he or she wants. Even if you give the person a list, you have no guarantee that your instructions will be followed or that they will even be accepted. A power of attorney offers benefits when properly used, but it is a *weak* legal document and should *never* be used as a primary estate plan to avoid probate.

Myth 5: "I can avoid probate by adding a transfer on death beneficiary on my property."

False! Transfer on death (also called "pay on death" or "TOD" or "POD") is now permitted in many states. Transfer on death is an old idea—life insurance policies have always let you designate a beneficiary. What's new is that the beneficiary concept is being expanded to include property such as bank accounts, stocks, cars, real estate, etc. For example, with real estate you sign a "beneficiary deed" naming the beneficiary and have it recorded. The beneficiary becomes the owner of the property immediately after your death without probate.

So far this sounds great. But what if you become incompetent? Your beneficiaries have no legal authority until *you*, the owner of the property, die. In the meantime, your beneficiaries cannot manage your financial affairs. They will have to request that the probate court declare you incompetent and put you into a conservatorship before they can take care of you.

Transfer on death doesn't always avoid probate at death either. If the owner and the beneficiary die at the same time or if the beneficiary dies before the owner, probate will occur. Probate will also be necessary if the beneficiary is incompetent when the owner dies. If the beneficiary is a minor child, then the property will go into a probate guardianship for the child.

Transfer on death is not an estate plan and it doesn't avoid probate. You have no control over the outcome, because it is not flexible enough to handle unanticipated events. And it is especially risky if the owner becomes incompetent.

Transfer on death is not an estate plan and it doesn't avoid probate

Doing Nothing: *No written instructions if you become incapacitated or die.*

Incapacity:	Probate. If you are unable to manage your affairs because of incapacity, only the probate court can do it for you through a conservatorship/guardianship.
Death:	Probate. All assets in your name must be probated before your heirs can receive them.
Type of law:	Controlled by probate law. Not a contract. Does not avoid probate.

Joint ownership: *Also called "joint ownership with right of survivorship." When two or more persons own the same asset. Not an estate plan.*

Incapacity:	Probate. If a co-owner becomes incapacitated the other co-owner may not be able to sell or refinance the assets without court approval through a probate conservatorship/guardianship.
Death:	Probate. Assets must be probated before going to the heirs of the last co-owner to die.
Liability:	Your assets are exposed to the creditor claims and lawsuits against the other co-owner.
Type of law:	Controlled by probate law. Not a contract. Does not avoid probate.

Power of Attorney: *Document giving someone legal authority to sign your name on your behalf. Ends at incapacity (unless it is a durable power of attorney) or death. Not an estate plan.*

Incapacity:	Probate. Can be rejected at any time for any reason.
Death:	Probate. All powers of attorney end when the signer dies.
Type of law:	Controlled by probate law. Not a contract. Does not avoid probate.

Transfer on Death: *Also called "pay on death," "TOD" or "POD." Naming a beneficiary on your assets.*

Incapacity:	Probate. Beneficiaries have no legal authority to care for an incapacitated owner or prevent him/her from going into living probate.
Death:	Probate, if the beneficiary dies with or before the owner, or is a minor.
Type of law:	Limited contract protection. Controlled by probate law. Does not avoid probate.

Will: *Document containing instructions for distributing your property after you die.*

Incapacity:	Probate. Only effective after you die. Provides no protection if you become incapacitated.
Death:	Will must be probated before assets can be distributed.
Type of law:	Controlled by probate law. Not a contract. Does not avoid probate.

Living Trust: *Also called a "revocable inter vivos trust." A legal document into which you place all of your assets, with instructions for their management and distribution upon your incapacity or death.*

Incapacity:	No probate. Your personally chosen backup trustee takes over and manages your affairs privately.
Death:	No probate. Your backup trustee pays your bills and distributes your property privately according to your written instructions. Probate court is not involved.
Type of law:	Controlled by trust law. Is a contract. Completely avoids probate.

In summary, now you know about the risks involved with the most common methods people use to try to avoid probate. A living trust eliminates all of these risks and completely avoids probate. It ensures that your estate plan will remain your plan, and that it can't be changed by the court, unanticipated events, or greedy relatives. Remember, probate can happen in three situations—when you die, if you become incompetent, and where minor children are involved. The information on the next few pages will help you to better understand each of these situations. To fully comprehend the important benefits of a living trust, you'll need to know exactly what happens during probate—to you, your family and your property.

WHEN YOU DIE

Whether or not you have a will when you die, the process to probate your estate (your possessions and debts at the time of your death) is virtually the same. Your family will not be able to change titles on property listed in your name without a court order—and this is done only through the probate court. This includes *any* titled property, such as bank accounts, stocks and bonds, real estate, and cars. Even if you have a will, a court order is still required because a will by itself is not enough authority to retitle property or release account balances.

THE PROBATE PROCESS

First, of course, you die.

Your executor (if you named one in your will) has not yet been formally appointed by the court and can take only limited actions at this point, such as notifying your employer and bank of your death, requesting cancellation of the utilities to your home, and cancelling magazine and newspaper subscriptions. If you didn't have a will, then a family member can take care of these things, but legally this is about all they can do at this time.

In addition, your family and/or friends cannot legally take any of your belongings before the probate process has been completed, unless they get specific approval from the court. In fact, there could be serious consequences if they do. You've probably seen or heard of relatives taking personal belongings and sentimental items immediately after the funeral. If it's your family, *don't do it*. And if you're named an executor, *don't let anyone else do it*. Several steps, which follow, must be taken before any property can be distributed to your heirs.

File Petition

Probate does not automatically start when you die. Someone must request that probate begin. This generally happens because checks need to be written from your bank account to pay bills and the account may be frozen, or your property needs to be sold, or your other assets need to be liquidated or transferred to a new owner or to your heirs. Usually a family member (when there is no will) or your executor (when there is a will) requests that probate proceedings begin. This is a formal legal process. A written petition, prepared by an attorney, is submitted to the court to start the proceedings and can include your original will (if you had one). A filing fee (paid from your assets) will be charged to your estate, usually when the petition is presented to the court.

Publication

After the petition is filed, in most states the court will order a formal notice to be published in a local newspaper for several weeks or months before the first hearing. This procedure notifies the public of your death, requests that your creditors present any unpaid debts to the court, and invites anyone who feels they have a right to part of your estate to come forward and make their claim. The cost of this advertising (usually several hundred dollars) is paid from the assets in your estate.

The executor is also required to send a *written notice* of your death to all of your *known* creditors, and to anyone else he/she thinks *may* have a claim against your estate.

At the same time, your executor notifies your named heirs of your death, sends each of them a copy of your will (if you had one), and advises them where the probate proceedings will be held. This is when everyone finds out how much they will (or won't) receive from your estate.

First Hearing

The first hearing is held six weeks to two months after the filing of the petition. Assuming there are no contests to your will or any other unusual circumstances, the following steps usually occur at this hearing:

Will is Validated

If you had a will, it must be validated by the court. The judge will make sure it meets the state's legal requirements—that it is the correct will (in case you left more than one), that you were in a competent state of mind when it was drawn up, that all the proper signatures are on it, that it was witnessed, and so on. If the judge rejects your will as invalid, then the court will declare that you died without a will and order the state's will applied instead.

Executor/Administrator Is Appointed

After the will is validated and *admitted* into probate, the court will formally appoint the executor (sometimes called a "personal representative") to manage your estate for the court. If you had a will, you may have named someone to be your executor. If this person is still alive and able to act in this capacity, the judge will probably accept your choice. If not, the judge will appoint someone else, usually a relative, but sometimes an attorney or a bank's trust department.

If you did not have a will, the court will appoint an "administrator" to perform these duties. (An executor and an administrator have the same responsibilities. To keep things simple, we will use the term executor when referring to this position from now on.)

Executor's Duties And Fees

The executor helps the court to inventory your possessions and determine their value. He/she is responsible for collecting your bills and preparing your final tax returns, and for presenting them to the court to be approved and paid. The executor also applies to Social Security, veterans, union or fraternal organizations, and other groups or organizations for any death benefits to which your estate is entitled. This includes death benefits from life insurance, IRA's, retirement plans, etc., where you named "my estate" as the beneficiary.

The court will grant your executor "letters testamentary." This is a legal document, an order signed by the judge, which formally appoints the executor and grants him/her the authority to act in your place under court supervision. These "letters" are what the bank and others need to close out your accounts and turn your assets over to your executor. In effect, the titles of your property transfer from you to your executor, who is responsible for their safekeeping while your estate is probated.

Executors are entitled to receive payment for their services and are often required to post a bond; normally both payments are made from the assets in your estate.

It is important to note that in many states the executor does not have the authority to act independently—every action is controlled and must ultimately be approved by the probate court. So, even though your estate is paying for his/her services, your executor is really working for the court.

Independent Administration

Some states permit independent or unsupervised administration, in which the executor's actions and records are not pre-approved by the court. This does reduce the amount of paperwork; but because the estate is still in probate, it remains a slow process. The requirements for independent administration vary in each state permitting it. In California, for example, the court can permit independent administration unless your will specifically states that you do not want it. In other states, you must specifically include in your will that you do want your estate to be independently administered, or *all* of your beneficiaries must agree to give the executor this unsupervised authority. It may be difficult to get them all to agree, especially if they live far apart.

Unusual Circumstances

If your will is contested or if there are any other unusual circumstances, the court will try to resolve them at this first hearing. If the differences cannot be resolved at this time, there will be additional hearings until the conflict can be resolved by the court. The court will decide if anyone who claims to be one of your "heirs" has a valid right to part of your estate, whether or not you included him or her in your will. It is not uncommon for these "heirs" to find out how much your estate is worth from the newspaper publications and court records, and then hire an attorney to contest the will—sometimes even when they have no real hope of getting anything. In many states the person contesting the will can have his/her attorney fees paid out of the estate, so the contesting party has nothing to lose. Because contesting a will can get very expensive and prolong probate, families quite often pay off contesting heirs just to get rid of them.

Also, since executors are entitled to be paid for their services, more than one of your relatives or friends may want this responsibility, resulting in more court hearings to determine who will actually be appointed by the court. This can significantly increase the time and cost of probate and could result in hurt feelings as well. Even if you specify an executor in your will, your choice can be contested.

File Opened/Attorney Appointed

At the end of the first hearing, the court will formally open a file on your estate and appoint an attorney to handle the estate's paperwork for the court. Although having an attorney is not always a legal requirement, it has become a practical necessity because probate paperwork and filing procedures can be extremely complicated. Also, judges prefer to deal with an attorney who understands how the probate system works. You may specify an attorney in your will, however, your family may ask for a different attorney or they may ask the court to select an attorney. Of course, all attorney fees are paid from the assets in your estate.

Assets Frozen/Inventory Estate

During probate, your assets are usually frozen so that an accurate inventory of your property and possessions can be taken. This means that your heirs cannot receive their inheritances, nor can any property or assets be sold or liquidated without the court's permission.

After the first hearing, the executor must locate all of your property and possessions, compile a list of them and their values, and present it to the court. This can be a very time-consuming and difficult process, especially if you did not have current and accurate records, or if you had assets in several states. The court will require formal appraisals (usually by a certified, court-approved appraiser) for many items such as real estate, antiques, collectibles, cars, art, furniture, etc. Appraisal fees can be expensive, and these are also paid from your estate.

Family Living Allowance

During this time, your dependents (spouse and minor children) will probably be granted a living allowance, but it must be "reasonable" and approved by the court. To request the allowance, your spouse must submit a written request to the court through the attorney. If there are a number of outstanding debts, or if the will is being contested, a judge may insist that the assets remain intact and reduce or even deny the request.

However, proceeds from assets with beneficiary designations (such as life insurance, IRA's, retirement plans) are paid directly to your beneficiary without probate, so your family will probably have some money for living expenses. And it's likely the court will allow your dependents to continue living in your home during probate, even if it will eventually go to someone else.

Presentation And Payment Of Debts, Claims And Taxes

Your creditors have a certain number of days from the first publication of notice of your death to come forward and submit their claims against your estate for payment. After this time has passed, the executor will audit the claims and present them to the court for approval to pay them from the assets in your estate. If there are any disputes over a claim, there could be additional hearings (at additional costs to your estate), with the judge making the final decision.

Final Distribution/Closing Of Estate

Finally, after the court is satisfied that the legal process has been completed—which commonly takes a year or more—it will order another public notice to announce a final hearing to close your estate. At this hearing, the judge will review all of the paperwork and order your debts, claims, taxes and probate expenses (including attorney and executor fees, probate fees, bonds, and appraisals) to be paid.

The cash assets in an estate can be greatly reduced, even consumed, due to the ongoing expenses of probate. If there is not enough cash in your estate to pay your debts, then the judge can order that your property, including your personal belongings, be sold at a public auction or estate sale. Many times this will be on a "distressed sale" basis for a fraction of its worth.

After all bills have been paid, the court will order your remaining property distributed to your heirs according to your will (or the state's will if you didn't have one). The judge will then order the executor relieved of his/her duties and the file closed.

Multiple Probate?

If you owned real estate (including condominiums, timeshare units, and oil, gas, or mineral rights) in more than one state, this entire process (and its expenses) may have to be repeated in each state where your real estate is located.

A Word About Very Small Estates

The only real exception to the process as we explain it here is that some states have a shortened probate process for *very small* estates. Estates that qualify can be probated without an attorney or executor fairly quickly and with just a minimum filing fee. But very few actually qualify for this

The probate process— not your family— has control

special process because the limits on the total estate value are extremely low—as low as $15,000 in some states. And if any creditor claims are presented, then the estate will probably have to go through regular probate anyway.

WHAT THE PROBATE PROCESS DOES TO YOUR FAMILY

Probate Is Expensive

There are many costs, often substantial, that must be paid from your estate—leaving less for your heirs.

Where Does The Money Go?

First of all, the probate judge does not directly take any of your money. Judges are paid from our tax dollars to enforce the laws. And the government doesn't take money directly from your estate when you die, unless it is large enough to have to pay estate taxes (also known as death taxes which we will discuss later in *Part Four*).

Before your heirs can receive any part of your estate, all expenses connected with the probate process must be paid. And there are many expenses—filing fees and court costs, publication and advertising expenses, appraisal and auction costs, bond fees, and attorney and executor fees.

Attorney And Executor Fees Are Hard To Predict

The biggest expense of probate is the attorney and executor fees, which can easily run into many thousands of dollars. Each state has its own method for determining these fees. Some states establish a guideline to help regulate fees, based on a percentage of the gross or net value of the estate, but a judge can (and often does) approve higher fees, based on individual circumstances and the time involved. Other states permit hourly fees—$125.00 to $250.00 per hour is not an unusual attorney rate. Often, the executor will receive a lower hourly rate, but some states specify that the executor will be paid the same rate as the attorney.

Most executors and attorneys are required by the court to keep a detailed record of the amount of time they spend on each case—telephone calls, letters, answering questions, court appearances, etc. So the more time they have to spend probating an estate, the more costly the probate process becomes.

So How Much Does Probate Cost?

Total probate costs are often estimated to be from 5% to 10% of an estate's *gross* value, which is the fair market value of an estate at death *before* any debts (including the mortgage on your home and other loans) have been paid.

In most states, probate fees are based upon the gross estate value. So if your home is worth $100,000 when you die, probate fees will based on $100,000, even if the mortgage is $75,000!

The following chart shows the attorney and executor fees in California, Missouri and Florida. These amounts do *not* include other probate expenses, such as publication and appraisal costs, filing and bond fees and additional legal fees (if your estate is complicated or your will is contested).

ATTORNEY AND EXECUTOR FEES

Gross Estate Value	Combined Minimum Fees For Attorney and Executor*		
	California	*Missouri*	*Florida*
$100,000	$6,300	$6,600	$5,000
$200,000	$10,300	$12,100	$10,000
$500,000	$22,300	$28,100	$25,000
$1,000,000	$42,300	$53,100	$60,000
$2,000,000	$62,300	$93,100	$115,000

Statutory minimum fees for California, Missouri and Florida. Does not include other probate fees such as filing fees, appraisals, publication fees, bonds, and legal fees for "extraordinary" services. Probate fees in your state may be higher or lower.

Probate costs frequently exceed the fee ranges given above. It is very common for the attorney and executor to request and receive additional fees, especially if there are extenuating circumstances involved. If your will is contested or ruled invalid by the court, attorney fees and court costs can escalate dramatically. If you own several real estate properties which have to be sold, the appraisal and publication costs will be more than an estate which has no real estate. If you die without a will, the court has to spend more time determining your heirs (enforcing the state's will) and deciding who will be your administrator. If you died and left small children, the court will have to establish a guardianship for them (which requires extra court hearings and testimony).

Every additional decision or transaction required to complete the probate process will increase the cost. It is virtually impossible to predict the final probate cost for any estate—there's just no way of knowing until the actual process has been completed.

But I Don't have That Much, So Why Should I Worry About The Cost Of Probate?

Probate can affect *any* size estate, large or small, and especially those with real estate. Because probate costs take a greater percentage from small estates than large ones, anyone with a smaller estate should not risk probate. There just isn't that much to go around in the first place.

Your Family Loses Control

As we mentioned earlier, during probate your family may not be able to sell property or liquidate assets without court approval, even if they need the money. The probate process, not your family, has control. Your family must function within the restrictions of the probate system. It can be very frustrating for your family when they have to pay for the court to tell them who gets what and when. You can understand how this can lead to all kinds of family disputes.

Probate Takes Time

Probate delays can also be extremely frustrating. Remember, the probate system was designed to be slow. It must follow legal procedures exactly, and this process is notoriously time consuming. Some of the time required for probate is very specific, such as how long the published notices of your death must run in the papers (in those states that require it) and how long your creditors have to present their claims.

Other parts of the process are totally unpredictable. For example, your executor may need additional time to get your affairs in order and to locate and inventory all of your assets. Of course, any complications (such as your will being contested) will create additional delays. But, in reality, a good portion of the time required for probate is due to the over-booked court system. Even if everything else runs smoothly, it may take several months just to get a court date. The probate process is slow, usually taking one to two years, often longer.

Probate costs average 5%-10% of an estate's gross value

Time Is Money

Your assets can depreciate while they are tied up in probate. Stocks, real estate and other assets can lose value if they cannot be sold quickly enough in a declining market. Your heirs could miss out on certain opportunities that require an immediate decision, such as buying a home or making an investment. Probate is a slow process and, in today's financial world, decisions must often be made quickly.

No Privacy

All probate proceedings are a matter of public record. In those states that require it, advertising notifies your creditors to present their unpaid bills, but it also encourages the interest and attention of those who may feel they have a right to part of your estate (whether or not they actually do). You may have purposely left some of your relatives out of your will, but they can contest your will and the court, not you, will decide if they are entitled to receive a share of your estate. Remember how many people claimed to be somehow "related" to Howard Hughes when he died?

Since it is public record, anyone can go to the probate court and find out the details of your estate. Jacqueline Kennedy Onassis was one of the most private women in the world, but her will did not protect her privacy. Anyone can look up the probate records and find out how she distributed her estate, including who received her copy of John F. Kennedy's Inaugural Address signed by Robert Frost, or that she left $500,000 to each of her sister's children. They can also see how much she left family members and friends and learn their addresses at the time of her death. Do you want just anyone to be able to find out what you owned, what you owed, and the amount you left to each of your heirs? Do you want their addresses to be available to the public?

In addition, there are people who go through probate records and compile lists of new widows and beneficiaries. These lists are then sold as leads to companies or individuals selling "investments," offering to "manage" finances, or other "helpful" activities. Some of these are legitimate, but many are outright scams—unscrupulous individuals who prey upon bereaved survivors, particularly spouses, who are at an especially vulnerable time in their lives. Many of these surviving spouses have never had to handle finances before. They are not only emotionally upset about the loss of their partner, but also are understandably terrified about being alone and on their own. If your family has to go through probate, then they could be exposed to possible exploitation.

Emotional Cost

Because it is an ongoing process, probate can be a frequent interruption, preventing your family from resuming their day-to-day activities and serving as a constant reminder of your absence. It can also cause unpleasant disagreements among family members who would normally look to one another for support.

A family is used to running its own affairs in private, according to its needs. You make decisions on a daily, even hourly, basis to accommodate different situations and personalities. But, probate rules and regulations are very rigid and the law cannot bend or make allowances for individuals. When it seems that nothing is happening, or that things are taking too long to resolve, it's often impossible for a family member to get answers. The court will not communicate directly with the family (a judge's duty is to enforce the law, not to give legal advice), so all communication regarding the estate must go through an attorney.

It's common for family and in-laws to become frustrated and, because they cannot vent their frustrations on the court, they may end up taking them out on each other. When people react emotionally instead of rationally, it's extremely difficult to reach an agreement, and then the court may have to get involved to settle what should have been a simple agreement worked out among caring family members.

It's Your Choice—But There's More!

If you're not already convinced that you need a living trust to transfer your property when you die, read a little further, because we're not through yet. Would you believe that the probate process can take control while you are still alive?

IF YOU BECOME INCAPACITATED OR INCOMPETENT

Most people usually associate probate with "something that happens when you die." Few know that the probate court can take control of your finances and personal affairs *before* you die!

If you are unable to manage your personal and financial affairs, then you will most likely be declared incompetent and placed under the control of the probate court in something called a "conservatorship" (also called a "probate guardianship" or "living probate")—especially if you own any titled property (home, other real estate, car, bank/savings accounts). This will affect both you and your family in ways you have never dreamed. Most people don't even think twice about the very real possibility of becoming incapacitated or incompetent at some time in their lives. It can happen to any of us, at any age. And if it does, you could be placed in a probate conservatorship, whether you have a will or not. Incapacitated and incompetent both mean that a person is temporarily or permanently unable to manage his/her own affairs. To keep things simple, we will, with a few exceptions, use the term "incapacitated" when referring to this condition from now on.

It is estimated that 30% to 40% of Americans will become incapacitated before they die. And with medical advances people are living longer, greatly increasing the possibility of accidents, senility and afflictions such as Alzheimer's disease (the disease that debilitated former President Ronald Reagan).

One thing is certain: most of us will, at one time or another, find ourselves faced with the care of an older relative (most likely our parents). And because most people are not prepared, many of us will have to deal with probate conservatorships when we try to take care of our elderly parents and relatives.

But not just older people end up in probate conservatorships. It can happen to any of us at any time—and at any age. Without warning, you could be critically injured in an accident or stricken with a devastating illness (physical or mental). You will be alive but without the capacity to handle your own affairs. If this happens, then you'll probably be placed in a probate conservatorship. Here's why:

Why A Will Won't Protect You

Many people think that if they have a will and become incapacitated, their spouse or adult children (or the person they named as executor in their will) can automatically take care of their day-to-day affairs. But a will can only go into effect *after* you die. It cannot help if you become incapacitated—because you haven't died.

What Is A Probate Conservatorship?

This is a legal process that was created to protect you and your property if you are unable to take care of your own affairs. The original intention was, of course, very honorable. To prevent someone from taking over your property and squandering your possessions, the court takes control, making financial decisions for you and looking after your welfare.

What's Wrong With It?

Today most people would prefer that a family member or friend, rather than the court, take care of them. But if you are placed under a probate conservatorship, the court does take over, and you and your family lose all direct control. You lose your legal rights as an individual and have no choice about how your money is spent or who will look after your care. Even if a family member is named as your guardian, the court will still control your money. And, just like probate at death, a conservatorship is expensive and time consuming.

HOW YOU CAN END UP IN A PROBATE CONSERVATORSHIP

If You Own Property In Your Name

If you own titled property (home, other real estate, car, bank/savings accounts, etc.) in your name only and you become incapacitated, someone will have to ask the court to act for you. Your family and friends cannot write checks for you and pay your bills to keep your financial affairs in order. If yours is the only authorized signature, the *court* must do it for you under a probate conservatorship. If any of your titled property must be sold for any reason, including to pay for your care, then only the probate court can sign your name to transfer the title.

The Consequences If A Joint Owner Cannot Sign

As we discussed on *Page 14*, if you own titled property jointly and you become incapacitated, the other co-owner will have to get approval from the probate court (by placing you into a conservatorship) before the property can be sold, refinanced or transferred—even if the other co-owner is your spouse.

Most married couples own their property jointly and they assume that if one of them becomes incapacitated, then the other can continue to take care of their personal and financial affairs without interruption. But look at what happened to Karen.

Bill and Karen, a young professional couple in their thirties, were successful and responsible adults. They made safe investments and planned carefully for their future. They owned everything jointly and even had wills leaving everything to each other. But in a split second their lives changed dramatically when Bill was in a tragic car accident and suffered extensive brain damage.

Karen could continue to write checks and pay their day-to-day bills because only one signature was required on their checking account. But soon the cash started running out, and Karen realized she needed to sell some of their investments—maybe even their house—to pay for Bill's care and the other expenses. Karen was unable to sell any of their jointly owned property without both signatures. Since Bill could not legally sign his name, the only way Karen could sell their property was to place Bill into a probate conservatorship and have the court sign *for* him. Bill's will was no help at all because he was still alive.

Karen had no idea how expensive and cumbersome this legal "protection" would be. Not only did she have to deal with Bill's situation and the effect of this tragedy on their personal lives, but she also had to deal with the court system. She was especially frustrated that she had to pay for the court to approve the sale of their own property and then get the court's approval on how Bill's share of that money was spent—even when it was used to pay their personal expenses and to take care of Bill! When Bill died more than five years later, Karen found herself back in probate court—this time to probate Bill's will.

The same thing can easily happen to you if you own property through joint ownership. Many older parents list their adult sons or daughters as joint owners on their property (especially real estate), believing they will avoid probate when they die. They mistakenly assume that their adult child will automatically be able to take over for them if they become incapacitated. Most people just don't know how easily joint ownership can lead to a probate conservatorship and they have no idea what it can mean.

THE PROBATE CONSERVATORSHIP PROCESS

This is what generally happens if you are placed in a probate conservatorship. Some steps, as you will see, are very similar to the probate process at death. But keep in mind that while the process is going on, *you are still alive*.

Petition The Court

The court must be petitioned by someone on your behalf to begin proceedings to determine if you are incompetent. Usually a relative or neighbor will hire an attorney to start these proceedings. Very often, because of your condition, you will not know anything about this. In fact, some states do not even require that you be told.

Your will can't help if you are incapacitated

Proceedings Advertised

In most states, a notice of the conservatorship proceedings will be advertised in the local papers to allow your creditors a chance to present any unpaid bills to the court. This also makes your situation public.

Competency Hearing

A hearing is held to determine if you are incompetent. In some states, you are not even required to be present and the judge bases his/her decision on reports and testimony. If the probate judge decides that you are incompetent, you become a "ward of the court" and immediately lose most of your individual rights as a citizen.

Conservator/Attorney Appointed

The judge will appoint a "conservator" to handle your affairs for you (pay your bills, etc.) and make sure you receive proper care. Usually the conservator is a relative, but the judge can appoint anyone as your conservator, even someone you may not want to take care of you. The court opens a conservatorship file on you, which is available to the public. Conservators are entitled to be paid for their services and are required to post a bond. The court will also appoint an attorney to take care of the required paperwork. All conservator and attorney fees, bonds, filing fees, etc., are paid from your assets.

Inventory Assets And Debts

The conservator makes a list of your assets and debts and submits them, along with a budget for your living expenses, to the court for approval. The court may order your property and personal belongings sold at public auction to help pay your expenses, including the costs of the conservatorship.

The Court Takes Control—Or Does It?

From this point, all of your affairs are handled by your court-appointed conservator, under the direct supervision of the court. Depending on the court system, your conservator may have to adhere to very strict monitoring and regulations, or may not be subject to much control at all.

If the court is very strict, all expenditures your conservator makes on your behalf (including medical care and even personal items, right down to toothpaste) must be documented and approved by the court, creating a lot of paperwork. Once a year, the attorney must submit a report of every financial transaction (including cancelled checks, receipts and bank statements). This report is audited and must be approved by the court, and it can take months to complete the process.

Other courts are not strict at all, usually because they do not have the resources to properly monitor the financial records. In these situations, the assets can (and often do) simply disappear without a trace—with no record of how the money was spent.

Ending A Conservatorship

It is very difficult and expensive to end a probate conservatorship (usually they continue until the person dies). If you recover and are once again able to take care of yourself, you must petition the court and prove your competency. You must hire an attorney to represent you, and you will probably have to hire at least one trained professional (physician, psychiatrist, psychologist, etc.) to confirm that you are now "well" and able to take care of yourself. Practically speaking, this could be difficult, if not impossible, to do. You may have a hard time convincing a judge that you are now competent when a court has already declared you incompetent.

Probate Again?

When you die, your family will have to go through probate all over again—this time to distribute your remaining assets to your heirs. A probate conservatorship only exists while you are alive; it does not replace probate when you die. So after your conservatorship file is closed (sometimes many months after your death), your remaining assets will be transferred to another court file, and the formal process we discussed earlier will begin.

HOW A PROBATE CONSERVATORSHIP AFFECTS YOU AND YOUR FAMILY

Because a conservatorship is conducted by the probate court, you and your family will be affected in many of the same ways as when an estate is probated at death. The process is still inflexible, expensive, and time consuming, but a conservatorship can go on indefinitely—until you either recover or die.

Probate files are open to the public

Financial Cost

All costs associated with your conservatorship—attorney and conservator fees, bonds, advertising, appraisals, filing fees, and court costs—are paid from your assets. These costs are unpredictable and can rapidly add up, especially if you require complicated medical care, have a lot of assets to manage or other special needs, and if the conservatorship continues for many years. The additional expense of a conservatorship can be especially hard on an older couple with a fixed income.

Don't forget the hidden costs. Your assets cannot be sold without the permission of the court, and real estate, stocks and other investments can quickly lose value while they are tied up in probate.

You And Your Family Lose Control

The court, not your family, makes all decisions for you—appointing your conservator, approving how your money is spent and determining the quality of your care. Even if someone in your family is appointed your conservator, the court will control and audit the financial records.

Takes Time

Since the court has to approve your expenses, this takes more time than if you are cared for *outside* the court system. Besides making sure you receive proper care, your conservator will have to spend additional time keeping up with the paperwork and satisfying the court's requirements. This could be especially difficult for an elderly spouse to handle if he/she is appointed as your conservator.

No Privacy

All probate proceedings are a matter of public record. Your personal and financial information is available for anyone to see even though you're still alive. You probably wouldn't want this information (and your condition) being made public.

Emotional Cost

This can be a very difficult time for your family. It's hard enough for most family members to adjust to the reality of your situation, and normally they want to take care of these matters *privately*. The conservatorship process only adds to their frustration. If the court orders your possessions sold at public auction to pay for your expenses, it could be an added emotional strain for your family to be forced to publicly sell your possessions while you are still alive.

Conservatorship Battles

The court must appoint your conservator, which can lead to a long and expensive court battle if more than one person wants to be your conservator, for any reason. Remember the Groucho Marx competency hearings, in which a woman friend of his tried to convince the court that he wanted her as his conservator? Although Groucho was living with this woman at the time and she had been taking care of him, the court appointed a relative as his conservator. The hearings were lengthy and very public—not a pleasant situation for any family to risk going through.

Potential For Abuse

As in Groucho's case, the court will usually appoint a family member as your conservator. But if you are alone and have no trusted relatives who live nearby, a scheming relative, associate or neighbor may find it very appealing to have you declared incompetent, have himself or herself appointed as your conservator, dump you into a nursing home and take control of your assets. Remember, the court may not even require you to be at the competency hearing.

And, as we mentioned earlier, you run the risk of being placed under the protection of a court that does not have the resources to properly monitor your conservatorship—leaving the door wide open to possible abuse.

Again, You Have A Choice

You can risk being placed in a conservatorship. Or you can get a living trust—and keep control of your affairs privately, even if you become incapacitated. It's your choice.

There is one more area in which probate can interfere with our intentions, and that's when a minor child inherits money or property.

MINOR CHILDREN AND PROBATE

When most people think about a court guardianship for a child, they think of a situation right out of a Charles Dickens novel, with the poor orphan caught between the lawyers, the court and the guardian. That's not so far off, even today.

But did you know that a child can be placed in a probate guardianship even when one or both parents are still alive? Minor children cannot legally transfer property titled in their names, because minors do not have full legal rights. So if a minor child is named as a joint owner of property or inherits titled property (including real estate, stocks, bonds, proceeds as beneficiary of life insurance or IRA's, etc.), then the court will have to get involved to protect the child's interests when the property is transferred or sold. Remember, only the court can sign for the child. Sometimes the court will get involved even *before* the child can receive the asset or be named on the title, depending on the value and type of property. This is not an unusual situation as we'll explain shortly.

HOW CHILDREN CAN BE PLACED IN A PROBATE GUARDIANSHIP

If Both Parents Die

This is the most obvious situation, but there are some issues here which might surprise you. Most parents think that if they name a guardian for their minor children in their will, then that person will automatically be able to take over upon their deaths and raise the child using the child's inheritance. But this is not what happens.

When your estate goes into probate after your death, the court must appoint a guardian for your child. If you named a guardian in your will, the court will usually go along with your choice to *raise* your child, but it doesn't have to. The court may appoint someone else if it decides that person would be better than your choice. Of course, if you didn't have a will, the court will make its decision without knowing your wishes.

But—*and this is very important*—the *court,* not the guardian, will keep control over the child's inheritance through a probate guardianship. The guardian will get custody of the child, but the court will have control of the money.

Why A Children's Trust In A Will Is Risky

Some people put a "children's trust" in their will to prevent the court from taking control of the inheritance. It will work, but probably not the way most people think, and it may not work when your children really need it.

First of all, because it is part of your will, a children's trust can only go into effect *after* your will has been probated. It is funded with your assets. Those with beneficiary designations (such as life insurance, IRA's, retirement plans, etc.) can be paid to your children's trust right away without probate if you have named your children's trust as the beneficiary. But other titled assets (especially real estate) will have to be probated first—and that takes time and costs money (you know the story by now). So it could be months or years before these assets can go into your children's trust.

Secondly, what happens if you become incapacitated due to an illness or accident? Since you haven't died, your children's trust can't go into effect because your will can't be probated. Not even the beneficiary proceeds can be paid because you're still alive. You will probably be placed in a probate conservatorship (along with your children if both parents are incapacitated or if you are a single parent).

Using a children's trust in a will does work eventually, but it doesn't avoid probate and it will *not* go into effect if you become incapacitated.

If Both Parents Are Not Dead

But what if the child is not an orphan? You may wonder how a child could possibly be placed in a probate guardianship if both parents are still alive. Surprisingly, this happens more often than you might think.

Inheritances

Many parents, as well as grandparents and other relatives, leave money, real estate, stocks, CD's, and other investments to a minor child when they die. If the child is still a minor when the estate is probated, the court will have to get involved, especially if the inheritance is substantial. The court has to make sure the child's interests are "protected," even if both parents are alive and well. Of course, this protection isn't free and the child's inheritance (or the parents) will have to pay for it. An attorney will need to represent the child in court, and the court will probably insist

The court, not the guardian, controls the child's inheritance

that a guardian (usually a parent) is added to the titles when they are transferred to the child.

Establishing a guardianship for a minor child is a relatively simple process, but once it is set up the court will stay involved. Until the child reaches legal age, none of the child's assets can be sold (nor the money spent) without the court's approval. And this guardianship can go on indefinitely if the child is incapacitated upon reaching legal age.

Joint Ownership With A Minor

Naming a minor as a joint owner of any titled property (real estate, stocks, bond, etc.) can have devastating consequences because the only way to transfer, sell or refinance the property is through a probate guardianship. Here is another case of good intentions gone wrong.

Luanne, who was recently divorced, added her 12-year-old son as joint owner on the deed to her house, thinking it would automatically become his if she died. A year later, she decided to sell the house. But she couldn't, because her minor son (her joint owner) could not legally sign the deed. She had to put her own son in a probate guardianship and the court had to approve the sale. By that time the buyers were long gone, but the court was still there. Eventually she was able to find another buyer and this time the sale went through. But the court kept control over her son's share of the proceeds until he turned eighteen—at which time he promptly spent it all! Luanne couldn't afford to buy another house with just her share. She found out the hard way that joint ownership with a minor does not work.

Incapacity

And, of course, if both parents become incapacitated (or if you are a single parent), then the parent(s) *and* the child will be placed into a court conservatorship/guardianship—even if you have a will and a children's trust in your will.

Minor Children As Beneficiaries

Here's something else you may not have thought about. Most life insurance companies (and other companies who provide assets with beneficiary provisions such as IRA's, profit sharing/retirement plans, etc.) will not knowingly pay death benefits directly to a minor child. They will usually require proof of a court approved guardianship, because they do not want the risk of legal liability. Obeying a court order eliminates any liability risk that could result from turning over large amounts of money to a minor. Many people are not aware of this and list their minor children as beneficiaries (either primary or secondary) on their life insurance policies and other accounts.

In summary, if you leave any titled property to your children or grandchildren, or name the child as a joint owner, or make the child the beneficiary of your life insurance, IRA, or profit sharing/retirement benefits, you could unintentionally create a probate guardianship for the child.

THE PROBATE GUARDIANSHIP PROCESS

A probate guardianship for minor children works about the same way as for adults who cannot handle their own affairs and have been put into a conservatorship. The child's court-appointed guardian will need to hire an attorney, post bond and submit a detailed accounting report to the court each year. Anything the child needs that costs money (including education, school and social activities, music lessons, clothes, etc.) must be submitted in a written request by the attorney and approved by the court. And, of course, the guardianship costs money, which is paid for from the child's inheritance.

Besides the financial costs, there can also be *emotional* costs. Guardians and the court can get into disagreements over what is and is not important for the child's welfare. For instance, the guardian may feel it is very important for the child's development to take music lessons or to attend certain social functions. But the court may feel these expenditures are unnecessary or even frivolous. And the child is caught in the middle (shades of Charles Dickens). How do you explain all of this to a child?

The guardianship will continue until the minor child legally becomes an adult (age 18 in most states). At this time, the child will have *full control* over all of his/her inheritance. Many parents do not feel their children are mature enough at this age to handle this financial responsibility and prefer that their child inherit at a later age or in installments (receiving some money at age 21, more at 25, and so on). But a court guardianship cannot continue after the child has reached legal age.

Remember, too, if the court is not able to properly monitor the guardianship and the wrong person is appointed guardian, the child's

A child can get caught in the middle

inheritance could disappear. Sadly, this does happen. An understaffed or lax court could attract someone who will *pretend* they are concerned about the child just to be named guardian—when all that person is really concerned about is the child's money.

How A Probate Guardianship Affects Your Child And Your Family

Financial Cost

All costs associated with the guardianship are paid from the child's inheritance. Since raising a child can present any number of special circumstances, these costs are unpredictable and will vary for each individual. Depending on the amount of the inheritance and the duration and cost of the guardianship, the child's inheritance may be greatly reduced by the time the child receives it.

You Lose Control

The court, not the guardian you named in your will, controls your child's inheritance. The court can also override your choice of guardian and appoint someone else to raise your child. Your child will receive the entire inheritance when he/she legally becomes an adult in your state—you have no alternative. A children's trust in a will does prevent the court from taking control of the inheritance and lets you leave specific instructions for how the money will be spent, when your children will inherit, etc. But remember, the will must be probated first, and this can't happen if you are incapacitated.

Takes Time

In addition to the time it takes to care for your child, the guardian will have to spend time dealing with the court—keeping accurate records, dealing with the attorney and satisfying the court's requirements. This additional responsibility can cause even the most sincere and conscientious guardian to make compromises. It may be easier to "stick to basics" that don't require more time and paperwork, than to put forth the extra effort required to get court approval for a child's special needs.

It also takes time for a court and attorney to react, so there is little flexibility and spontaneity when it comes to your child's needs. And this complicated and time consuming process can easily frustrate the guardian causing him/her to feel some resentment towards the child, especially if the guardian has family responsibilities of his/her own.

No Privacy

Remember, all probate proceedings are public record, so anyone can find out the value of your child's inheritance and see how it is being spent.

Emotional Cost

Within a family, each child is recognized as a unique individual with his/her own identity and needs. But, under the law, the court must treat everyone equally, making it difficult for the court to make exceptions and address the special needs of each individual child. Also, any disputes between the guardian, attorney and court could have a negative impact on a child who has already lost his or her parents.

A Word Of Caution To Divorced Or Separated Parents

If your child's other natural parent is living at the time of your death or incapacity, the court will probably appoint him/her as your child's guardian, even though you may prefer someone else. Guardians are entitled to be paid for their services (from your child's inheritance), and this may be an incentive for your "ex" to be interested. What's more, if the court does not monitor the guardianship carefully, you run the risk of your "ex" having access to money that you intended to be used only for your child's welfare.

You Have A Choice Here, Too

You can do nothing, you can have a will, and you can even have a will with a children's trust in it—but you still risk having a probate guardianship for your minor children. A living trust will enable you to provide for your minor children, and *make sure* the court does *not* get involved even if you become incapacitated.

SO, THAT'S PROBATE!

You can see now why it's so important that you understand probate. Knowing that probate can take control when you die, if you become incapacitated, or if you have minor children and seeing how it can impact you and your family, whether you are married or single, young or old, will help you make the right choices in protecting your estate.

If the risks don't bother you, or if you really don't care about what probate can do, then you can still rely on the more commonly used methods for transferring property at death—wills (yours or the state's), joint ownership, or transfer on death. You can also give away all of your property while you are still alive. At least now you know the risks (and the costs) involved with these methods—*before* your family gets caught in the middle of probate.

But if you want to completely avoid probate, keep reading. Now we can tell you all about a living trust—what it is, how it works, how it avoids probate—and how your living trust can protect you and your family from unnecessary financial and emotional hardship.

With a living trust you can completely avoid probate—when you die, if you become incapacitated and when minor children are involved.

WHAT IS A LIVING TRUST AND HOW DOES IT AVOID PROBATE?

There are many different kinds of trusts. The legal name for the living trust discussed in this book is a "revocable inter vivos trust." It is also called a "revocable grantor trust." *Inter vivos* means that it is created during your lifetime. *Revocable* means that it can be revoked or changed.

A living trust is a legal document that allows you to transfer ownership of your titled property (home, other real estate, car, checking/saving accounts) and your personal property (clothes, furniture, jewelry) from your individual name to something called a "trust," which *you* control. Think of it as forming your own company, with you and your spouse as the only employees. You don't personally own your property anymore because everything is now owned by your new company (your trust). But you, as the owner of "your company," still have complete control over it.

You should know that a living trust is a *legal contract*. It is controlled by "trust law" which is a part of the law of contracts. By comparison, a will is *not* a contract and is controlled by probate law—which is completely separate from trust law. Every state has both trust laws and probate laws. Probate law *requires* the court to be involved. Trust law allows your business to be handled privately, even though you are incapacitated or dead, without any need for court involvement.

The United States Constitution guarantees that a living trust, which is valid in the state where it is set up, must be recognized by every state. In an age where people frequently relocate and often own assets in other states, a living trust gives you far more protection and flexibility than does probate, which is handled on a state-by-state basis.

Remember when we said there are only two ways to avoid probate—own nothing in your own name or have a living trust? A living trust lets you own nothing in your name, yet have complete control over everything in your trust name. *Nothing changes except the names on the titles.* Because it is a living trust, you continue to control everything just as you did before. This is *not* just a legal technicality. Adding your trust name on titles and beneficiary designations removes that property from probate law and places it under trust law. This is what keeps you and your family out of probate. Since you no longer own anything in your own name, and since your assets are no longer controlled by probate law, there is nothing to probate when you die or become incapacitated.

Living trusts are not new, and they are not tax shelters or gimmicks. They do not need to be complicated or expensive. And just about everyone—married or single, old or young—can benefit from a living trust, especially if you have children or own property. A living trust is particularly beneficial for single parents and unmarried persons.

If you want to make sure your loved ones (spouse, children, grandchildren, parents and trusted friends) will not have to deal with probate if something happens to you, then you should have a living trust. Just ask any experienced bank officer, stock broker, attorney, financial planner, CPA or life insurance agent. Or ask a history teacher.

History Of The Living Trust

History Of The Living Trust

The legal principles embodied in the modern living trust can be traced back to Roman law. The legal term "trust" comes from the English word "use," which is derived from the Latin word "opus" or "ad Opus." (In Old French, "opus" becomes "os" or "oes.")

These ancient trust terms are found in the oldest English and French trust documents. The Leofric and Godiva trust is a good example of this. The "charter" from Leofric, Earl of Mercia and his wife, the infamous Lady Godiva, (yes, the one who, according to legend, once rode naked on horseback through a crowded marketplace) was written around A.D. 1055. It is a type of early English "trust" or "use."

In it, the Earl and his wife are transferring certain property to the St. Mary Monastery at Worcester "for the use of its brethren." This document represents more than a simple gift or transfer of property. The Monastery is to hold title to the property for the benefit of its monks on the condition the monks say prayers for the souls of the Earl and his Lady. Furthermore, the property cannot be sold, transferred or used by anyone except the monks.

If the monks had stopped saying the required prayers, the laws of that time would have forced the monks to perform their prayer duties or return the property to the Earl or his heirs. No doubt, the monks had legal rights to protect themselves as well, such as keeping the monastery's abbot from backing out of the agreement or converting the property to another use. For example, in 1185, Pope Urban III ruled that a bishop holding property which had been given to the Church for a specific use could not divert the property to other Church purposes. The Bishop was "entrusted" to enforce the special instructions restricting the use of the donated property.

Here it is declared in this document that Earl Leofric and his wife have granted two estates, for the love of God and the sake of their souls, to the refectory of the holy foundation, the monastery of St. Mary at Worcester, for the use of the brethren who daily serve God therein, on condition that they intercede for our souls. Our gift comprises five hides of land at Wolverley and two at Blackwell and a messuage in the town, and it shall freely belong to their refectory for all time, and no one shall alienate it. And if there is anyone who desires to augment or endow it in any way, God Almighty shall grant him a prosperous life and eternal reward; and if, on the other hand, anyone is puffed up and so greatly covetous of earthly things that he desires to alienate this our gift, he shall have the curse of God and St. Mary and St. Oswald and all men in holy orders here in this life, and he shall be excommunicated on the Judgement Day in the presence of the Lord by God and by all his saints, and tormented for all time in everlasting punishment along with Judas and his companions, unless he desist and turn to a proper mode of conduct. And both of us shall be the protectors and guardians of these estates, on behalf of the holy monastery, as long as our life lasts.

Grant Of Land To Worcester By Leofric, Earl Of Mercia, And His Wife

Translation: Robertson, A.J. Ed., Anglo-Saxon Charters, Cambridge: Cambridge Univ. Press, 1956.
Photograph: Courtesy of The British Library, London, England.

The Leofric document resembles a living trust in several ways. There is a transfer of property with conditions attached to another person, the abbot of the St. Mary monastery, who is to hold title for the use of the monks of that monastery. Unlike modern living trusts, however, this was a simple one; it did not involve splitting the legal and equitable ownership. The monastery was simply to hold the property for its own members, the monks, on the condition they said prayers for the souls of Earl Leofric and Lady Godiva.

As early as the ninth century, there is evidence of more complex trusts. But this type of "use" did not become common until 1224, with the arrival of the Franciscans in England. Under the rules of their mendicant order, the Franciscans' vow of poverty prohibited owning property. But like all organizations, they needed material things in order to carry out their mission, especially land and dormitories for their monks.

Faced with this dilemma, the Franciscans came up with a very innovative concept. The trust they created allowed property to be transferred to a municipal corporation

History Of The Living Trust

(a City) which would hold title to the property for the use and benefit of the Franciscans. The Franciscan "use" contained all of the characteristics found in the modern living trust:

The person donating property made the transfer during his/her lifetime and in effect became the trust creator, now commonly referred to as the trust settlor, grantor or trustor.

The municipal corporation became the trustee holding "legal" title to the property, subject to the special instructions the trust creator included in the trust document.

The Franciscans became the beneficiary. As the equitable owners of the trust, they enjoyed all of the practical benefits of ownership, such as the right to possess and receive income from the property. From a strict technical standpoint, however, they were faithful to the rules of their order because they did not legally own anything. The municipal corporation actually held legal title as their trustee.

The Franciscans' ingenuity effectively solved their problem and simultaneously created the modern living trust.

The Franciscan "use" quickly spread to private landowners throughout England who copied the legal formula for reasons that had nothing to do with religion.

Landowners began using the Franciscan living trust idea in order to protect themselves and their families from the king's outrageous tax system. Horrendous taxes were owed to the king whenever land was transferred or when the owner died, became incapacitated, or happened to be a minor child. Perhaps this era gave rise to the time-honored phrase, "'use it or lose it."

By conveying their land to a "trustee" for the use and benefit of "others," many of the most grossly unjust taxes could be reduced or eliminated. A landowner could also circumvent legal restrictions which made it very difficult to "will" land outright to his children or to his wife. The trust kept family business out of the king's court system, which was very complicated, time consuming, and expensive.

English law (called "common law"), which included the living trust,

later became the basis for America's legal system. The living trust continued to work the same way—it kept family business out of the probate court (which replaced the king's court). It is recognized in all 50 states.

Back To Modern Times

The living trust was used centuries ago for many of the same reasons it appeals to families today. It allows families to manage their affairs privately in the event of incapacity or death without any involvement of the probate court. It protects minor children from a probate guardianship. And it can help reduce or eliminate taxes. Now more than 750 years old, the "modern" living trust is a reliable and traditional legal alternative. When properly prepared and implemented, it totally avoids all probate.

Today, instead of giving title to your property to the church, you give it to your trust. A living trust actually looks a lot like a will and, in fact, it actually does what many people assume a will does—it lets your property be distributed to the people or organizations you specify. But because it is under trust law, it does not go through probate. And a living trust does much more, as we'll explain in this section.

HOW A LIVING TRUST WORKS

A living trust contains three positions; the grantor, the trustee, and the beneficiary.

1. The Grantor

This is the person setting up the living trust—*you*. If you and your spouse are creating one trust together, you are the co-grantors of your trust. The grantor is also called the *settlor, trustor, or creator.* Legally, the grantor "owns" the trust and has the power to change or revoke the trust at any time.

2. The Trustee

You will name a trustee who will control and manage the assets in the trust. You can name yourself or anyone you want.

While you are living, you will probably want to be your own trustee so that you can continue to run your own affairs as long as you are able. If you are married, you and your spouse will probably be co-trustees. This way, either of you can automatically act for the other (just like a joint checking account) and, if one of you becomes incapacitated or dies, the other *instantly* has control of all trust property—*with no court involvement.* Remember, with a living trust, *neither* of you owns the property. Your trust does, and you own your trust.

Perhaps you don't want to be your own trustee. You can name an institution, such as bank or trust company (also called a corporate trustee) to act as your trustee, or your can name another person such as an adult family member or trusted friend.

The Back-Up Trustee

You will also name someone you know and trust as your back-up trustee (also called "successor trustee") if you are a single trustee, or in case something happens to both you and your spouse. In order to carry out your instructions, your back-up trustee will need only a copy of your death certificate or a letter from your personal physician if you are incapacitated, a copy of your trust document, and personal identification to verify that he/she is the person you named to be trustee in your place.

How Do You Know Your Back-Up Trustee Will Follow Your Instructions?

Under the law of trusts, trustees are "fiduciaries"—which means they have a legal duty to follow your trust instructions. Trustees must act at all times in a *prudent* (careful and conservative) manner for the benefit of the beneficiaries. Also, because a trust is a *legal contract,* a trustee is legally obligated to safeguard the trust assets and follow its instructions. This means that if your back-up trustee abuses his/her duties, then he/she is personally liable to the beneficiaries and can be removed as trustee.

Of course, trustee problems can be avoided by naming persons you trust absolutely. You can also name co-back-up trustees to act together, such as an adult son and daughter or an adult child and a corporate trustee. If you don't have any trustworthy family members or close friends, then naming a corporate trustee is a good choice.

Know also that a properly prepared living trust will provide checks and balances on back-ups, such as requiring your back-up trustee (when they start acting on your behalf) to keep your other back-ups informed of all financial transactions.

In summary, your acting trustee has very broad powers, but he/she always has a legal responsibility, under the law of trusts, to carry out your instructions.

3. **The Beneficiary**

Your beneficiaries in a living trust are the persons and/or organizations who will receive your trust property and personal effects when you die. Beneficiaries are usually family members and relatives, but you can leave your property to anyone or any organization you choose. You may wish to name a favorite charity, religious, educational or fraternal organization.

The Alternative Beneficiaries

You also need to name alternative beneficiaries in case your primary beneficiaries have died or are not in existence when you die.

What Happens If You Become Incapacitated

Your back-up trustee (or co-trustee) automatically takes over and handles your financial affairs for you. He/she can write checks, make deposits, apply for disability benefits, pay bills, sell property—anything necessary to keep your financial and personal affairs in order. No courts, attorneys or conservatorships are required and everything is done privately. You and your family are spared the entire frustrating, time consuming and expensive process of having to set up a probate conservatorship to get the court's approval to take care of you.

Plus, you have peace of mind knowing that, if this should ever happen to you or your spouse, you will be taken care of by someone you have selected, someone you know and trust—not someone a court appoints to take care of you. If you recover, you simply start handling your affairs again and your back-up trustee returns to being your back-up. There is no complicated paperwork or procedure required to regain control.

What Happens When You Die

Your back-up trustee (or co-trustee) will act essentially as an executor would if you had a will—but does *not* have to report to the court. He/she pays your final bills (signing checks now as the trustee for your trust) and then follows your instructions for distributing your assets to your beneficiaries. Your back-up trustee can even sell property, if that's what you wanted. Since all of your property is titled in the name of your trust, it's very easy for your back-up trustee to conduct business. The process is much quicker, less expensive and more private than probate. Your assets are *not* frozen and nothing is advertised, so no "heirs" are invited to make claims on your estate.

What Happens If You Have Minor Children

If you have minor children, you will need to set up a "children's trust" (also called a "testamentary trust" because it becomes effective after you die) *within your living trust* to prevent the court from taking control of the inheritance. Here's why. At the deaths of both you and your spouse, your back-up trustee will distribute your property and dissolve your trust. If you have minor children, then your trust needs to specify that their inheritance goes immediately from your trust into one for your children. The children's trust "inherits" *for* your minor children—they do not directly receive the inheritance in their own names. This is what keeps the court from taking control of the inheritance through a probate guardianship. As long as the inheritance stays in a trust—first in yours, then in one for your children—you will avoid probate.

In your children's trust, you name a *trustee* to manage your children's inheritance and a *guardian* to raise them according to your written

A living trust avoids all probate

instructions. The trustee and guardian can be the same person or different people. The court must still approve the guardian, but this is only a minor formality when compared to a probate guardianship in which the court also controls the inheritance. The court *cannot* overrule your choice of trustee, who will use the assets in the trust to care for your children until each reaches the age you specify. And with your hand-picked trustee controlling the money, there may be no real incentive for an irresponsible "ex" to want custody of your children.

Unlike a children's trust in a will, a children's trust within a living trust will automatically go into effect at death of the parents without probate. There will be no courts, attorneys or probate guardianships involved with your children's inheritance. And your trustee and guardian will have much more flexibility and will be able to respond more quickly to your children's changing needs than if a probate guardianship were involved. You can also use a "children's" trust within your living trust to leave an inheritance to your grandchildren or other family members.

HOW A LIVING TRUST IS SET UP

An attorney prepares your living trust based on *your* decisions about what you want to happen if you become incapacitated and when you die. *You* make the basic planning decisions, and you inventory your property, decide who you want to receive it when you die, name someone you trust to be responsible for its distribution, and someone to take care of you if you can no longer take care of yourself.

The attorney will make sure the living trust satisfies your state's legal requirements and will prepare it for you to sign. Trust documents are usually prepared from a standardized trust format. Because living trusts are traditional and well-established in estate planning, your attorney will not need to create something from scratch. In fact, most people only need one basic trust document to handle all their needs and property. This may sound pretty simple, and it is, as long as you use an attorney who is experienced in preparing living trusts estate plans and can make the necessary modifications to handle *your* family's situation. It is very important that your living trust be done properly.

After your attorney has prepared your living trust document and you have read and approved it, you sign the trust and have it notarized. You then put the trust name on the titles and account names of all of your titled property (real estate, checking and savings accounts, safe deposit box, investments, cars) and your beneficiary designations (insurance, IRA's, Keogh Plans, annuities). We'll explain this in a moment.

You Must Transfer All Property Into Your Trust Name

If you don't properly retitle your property and beneficiary designations into your trust name (also called "funding your trust"), then the assets are outside of the trust and could be probated. Just listing your property in your living trust is *not* enough—the trust name *must* be on the titles and beneficiary designations. Failure to properly retitle your property will cause the trust to fail (either partially or totally). Remember, the *only* way to completely avoid probate is to put *everything you own* into your living trust.

With the exception of real estate deeds (usually prepared by your attorney), we strongly recommend that *you* handle the retitling of your property yourself. This will save you money and make you familiar with the process. Your attorney should provide you with detailed written instructions for retitling your assets and authorization forms for you to complete and give to the companies with whom you do business. There should be no cost, except a nominal fee for recording your deed or reissuing your car title.

Not all companies are familiar with living trusts. And a few resist changing their ways to handle living trusts. If, for example, your bank doesn't want to rent your safe deposit box in your trust name, then we recommend you move your business to a bank that will. When faced with the loss of your business, it's remarkable how many companies suddenly discover that they can accommodate your request after all. Many living trust attorneys will "go to bat for you" at no additional cost if you need help. You shouldn't have any problems, but if you do, stand your ground and don't let someone talk you into doing something different. Remember, this is *your* property and *your* family. Don't compromise and jeopardize the probate protection provided by your living trust.

Finally, be suspicious if anyone tells you that you only need to put one asset or a "token" cash amount (twenty-five dollars seems to be most common) into your living trust to fund it. Single asset or "token amount" funding may be appropriate with *other* kinds of trusts, but this is *not* what you should do with your *living* trust. The only way your trust can completely avoid probate is for you to put *all* of your property into it.

Changing the names on titles is really simple to do, especially if you are working with an experienced living trust attorney who provides you with the instructions and forms needed to retitle your property.

Your attorney can verify the exact wording you should use, but your trust name will probably be similar to the following:

If you are single:

"Your name," Trustee under trust dated **"insert the date you signed your trust."**

Example: John W. Smith, Trustee UTD March 14, 1995.

If you are married:

"Your name, your spouse's name," Trustees under trust dated **"insert the date you signed your trust."**

Example: James C. Culver, Mary E. Culver, Trustees UTD January 19, 1995.

The designation "UTD" is often used as a shortened version of "under trust dated." Some companies use the designation "UAD," meaning "under agreement dated."

The use of "and" or "or" between acting trustee names.

A properly prepared trust will permit each original acting trustee to sign without the signature of the other. Government regulations frequently require specific wording for trust titles. For example, companies regulated by the FDIC (banks and savings and loans) require the word "or" be used between the trustee names, while companies regulated by the SEC (brokerage companies, etc.) require the word "and." Let the company insert whatever word they require so each original acting trustee can sign without a co-signature. Realize that some companies will still require all acting *competent* trustees to sign.

Titled Property

Almost any kind of property can be held in your trust including property you own in other states. Typical trust property includes real estate (like your home) and other property with formal titles (checking and savings accounts, stocks, bonds, mutual funds, cars). Some assets such as notes and mortgages payable to you, contracts for deed, leases, patents and copyrights, and partnership interests—can be *assigned* to your trust without actually retitling them. Your attorney can prepare assignment forms for you.

If you keep your investments with your broker in a "custodial" account (also called a "street name" or "trading" account), then the account is simply retitled to your trust name. Any original certificates you have for your investments will be reissued in your trust name. Rather than taking actual possession of original stock certificates, you may have your banker or broker keep your stocks or bonds in a custodial account for you in the name of your trust. This is much faster and easier and, since most brokers and bankers are insured, you don't have to worry about the certificates being misplaced or destroyed.

Most other types of assets can easily be handled by you with detailed instructions from your attorney. We will briefly discuss some of the most common assets to introduce you to this process.

Insurance

Mortgage, Credit Life, Health

Mortgage and credit life insurance pays off your mortgage or consumer loan should you (the borrower) die. There is no need to do anything with this type of insurance as long as the proceeds go directly to your lender only. Health insurance covers you *individually* and does not need to be put into your trust.

Liability, Casualty

Liability policies, such as homeowners or automobile insurance, should name your trust as an *additional insured*, so your policy covers you individually and as trustee of your trust.

Group, Employer Benefit

Life insurance which is a benefit through a group or your employer is usually a part of a master policy held by your employer, union, etc. If so, then you can only change the *beneficiary* to your trust because you do not "own" the group policy.

Life Insurance

Make your trust the owner of your life insurance policies. This way, if you become incapacitated, then your back-up trustee can borrow on the cash value of the policy (if needed) to help pay for your care. Name your trust as the primary beneficiary so the death proceeds are controlled by your trust plan when you die.

Beneficiary Designations

You should change all of your beneficiary designations (such as your life insurance policies) to the name of your trust, even though death proceeds are generally paid directly to the beneficiary without probate.
Here's why:

If your beneficiary is incapacitated when you die, the court will set up a probate conservatorship (or guardianship in the case of a minor child) on his/her behalf and control the proceeds—even if you have a living trust. But if your trust is listed as beneficiary, the death proceeds will be paid to your trust, and your back-up trustee will be able to use the funds to care for your beneficiary—without court involvement.

Here's something else to consider. What if you and your beneficiary die at the same time, or your beneficiary dies before you? Unless you have named a contingent beneficiary, the probate court will have to determine who receives the proceeds. These problems can be avoided by naming your trust as the beneficiary so *all* of your property and death proceeds are distributed according to your trust instructions. This is an efficient way to totally control your estate plan through one document—your living trust.

Finally, many people name "my estate" as their beneficiary. "My estate" means pay the proceeds directly to the probate court. In other words, until the court decides, no one really knows who is legally entitled to participate in your estate. As we previously explained, the probate court will collect the proceeds and distribute them, together with any other probated property, *after* the probate process is finished. Your beneficiaries will have to wait much longer to receive whatever proceeds are left after the probate costs are paid.

Real Estate

A quit claim deed is required to put real estate into your trust. For example, let's say you signed your trust on January 1, 1995 and your home is jointly titled in the names of both you and your spouse—"John and Mary Doe, husband and wife." To change the title to your trust, you and your spouse will sign a "quit-claim deed to living trust" (also called a "correction deed" or "trust transfer deed"), changing the title to *"John and Mary Doe, Trustees under trust dated January 1, 1995,"* and record the deed. That's all there is to it. If you later decide to sell your house, then your real estate broker (or the title company) would prepare a trustee's deed which you would sign as *"John and Mary Doe, Trustees under trust dated January 1, 1995."*

The reason you use a quit claim deed is that you are simply *correcting the title*—you are not *selling* the property. Remember, a living trust is revocable: you can always change your mind about any property you put into it. This is very different from selling, which is an irrevocable action. In most states, this will not trigger a reevaluation of your property taxes or disturb your current mortgage in any way. Your attorney can tell you how to do this or can do it for you. Most living trust attorneys prepare the quit claim deed to change the title of your home (and any other real estate you own) when they are setting up your trust. Just make sure he/she understands you want a *correction* of title, not a *transfer* of title.

Transferring real estate into a living trust requires a special type of quit claim deed. If the deed is not worded correctly, then unnecessary transfer taxes and other problems can result. To avoid problems, we recommend that you have your attorney prepare any necessary deeds. (Just make sure he/she is thoroughly familiar with living trusts.) The cost of a living trust estate plan should include the preparation of at least one deed for your home. If you have additional properties, then more deeds will be required so be sure to get a cost estimate in advance. Your attorney can handle the recording of your deed or you can do this yourself. Your attorney should provide you with instructions on how to record your deed, even for real estate in other states.

Make sure you immediately record your deed(s). You could have real problems if an unrecorded deed is lost, misplaced or destroyed.

Real estate is a big part of most estates and it is very important that it be correctly titled in your trust name. We are including this information in this section because a properly prepared living trust includes deed preparation and recording instructions.

Some mortgage companies prefer titles in the name of an individual instead of a trust, especially when refinancing a piece of real estate. Many mortgages are re-sold to institutions in the secondary lending market who may not buy mortgages in the name of a trust. They are concerned that some trusts may have special restrictions preventing a trustee from mortgaging or selling the property. Also, some mortgage company employees may not be familiar with living trusts. Rather than trying to educate them, it may be easier for you to transfer the title back to your name temporarily (until the loan has been approved and closed) and then to put it back in the name of your trust. However, you should know that federal regulations now allow residential lenders to refinance real estate that is titled in the living trust name. This is more convenient and less expensive.

A Special Note About Tax Deferred Investments

The most common tax deferred investments are IRA's (Individual Retirement Accounts), Keoghs, 401(k) plans, and *qualified* annuities. You did not pay any income tax on the money when it was deposited. The taxes are deferred until you later withdraw the money, usually after you've retired when hopefully your income and tax bracket are lower. Tax deferred investments *must* be individually owned and identified by the owner's social security number. Making a living trust the owner of a tax deferred plan will disqualify it (the trust does not qualify as an individual) causing the deferred income taxes to become due.

Connect your tax deferred investments to your living trust by naming the trust as a *beneficiary*. If you are married, name your spouse *individually* as the primary beneficiary and make your trust the *contingent* (or secondary) beneficiary. This allows your spouse (if he/she survives you) the option of "rolling over" the proceeds into his/her IRA, further deferring payment of income taxes. If you both die at the same time or if your spouse does not survive you, then the death proceeds are paid to your trust and distributed according to your plan.

Single persons cannot use the roll-over option, so the living trust is the primary beneficiary. Proceeds paid to your trust at your death may be immediately taxable, but your trust may be eligible for income averaging, which spreads the income and tax liability over several years. On the contrary, having the death proceeds paid outside of your trust risks probate because the proceeds are not controlled by your trust instructions.

Untitled Property

Many types of property, such as jewelry, art, clothes, and home furnishings, do not have formal title documents. You do not have to inventory or list these to include them in your trust. The standard provisions of a properly prepared living trust will automatically "assign" all of your untitled property and personal belongings into your trust when you sign it.

Property Acquired Or Sold After You Sign Your Trust

It is easy to put property acquired *after* you sign your trust into your trust name. For titled property just have the deed, title, policy or account set up in the name of your living trust when you acquire the property or open the account. For real estate have the seller deed the property directly to you as trustee of your trust. No special procedures are required, there is no need to change your trust documents, and you should not have any additional costs.

Untitled property works the same way. Suppose you buy a new sofa a year after signing your trust. Pay for it with a check drawn on an account titled in your trust name. The sofa automatically becomes a part of your trust; your cancelled check is proof of the purchase; and no special forms or lists are required. You don't have to do anything with your trust document.

If you sell or give away trust property, then it is automatically removed from your trust because your trust doesn't own it any more. Nothing else has to be done.

Loans and Debts

Debts that you owe, such as personal loans, credit cards, utilities, and mortgages, do not have to be retitled in trust name, because you (and your trust) continue to be obligated to pay them.

ADVANTAGES TO YOU AND YOUR FAMILY

Avoid Probate Costs

Avoiding probate will save your estate money, no matter what size estate you have. With a living trust, your estate pays $0 to lawyers and $0 to the court upon your incapacity or death. That's money in the bank for you and your heirs—where it belongs.

You Keep Control

The trust document outlines your instructions for managing your assets and distributing them after your death or if you become incapacitated. So even when you cannot handle your own affairs, you will be sure they are handled the way *you* want. Until that happens, you can sell trust property, change your beneficiaries, make new investments, or even cancel the entire trust at any time, for any reason. You can do everything you did before you set up the trust. You'll actually have more control with a living trust than you do now.

Takes Less Time

Distribution of your property when you die can usually be done in just a few weeks (larger estates may take a little more time), instead of months or years. If you become incapacitated, then your back-up (or co-trustee) immediately takes control for you. There are no court delays or interferences.

Maintains Your Privacy

A living trust is a private document. If you become incapacitated, then it will remain a private family affair. When you die, no announcements have to be placed in the newspaper, therefore no one is invited to contest your estate plan. Furthermore, your private plans will not be part of any public court record. No information about your assets, beneficiaries or trustees will ever be made public. It is so private that disgruntled relatives or opportunity seekers who might have contested your will may not even know you have died.

Difficult To Contest

A living trust *can* be contested, but not nearly as easily as a will. With a will, *anyone* can come forward and claim to have a right to part of your estate. But to contest a trust the left-out "heir" must hire a lawyer and file a *civil suit*, because trusts are controlled by contract (or civil) law, not probate law. Since the assets are not frozen under a living trust (as they are with a will), the trustee can go ahead and distribute them to the beneficiaries. The individual who wants to claim a piece of your estate must then sue each beneficiary, which is expensive and time consuming (especially if they live in another state). This process will usually discourage even the greediest "would-be heir" from contesting your wishes. As a practical matter, a properly prepared living trust is almost impossible to successfully contest.

Minimize Emotional Stress

With the court restrictions removed, your family can continue its normal day-to-day routines. All of your affairs can be handled quickly and easily. If you are incapacitated, then your family can look after your care privately. And when you die, they can grieve your passing privately and get on with their own lives without the frustration of prolonged court proceedings.

Inexpensive (And Easy) To Set Up

Expect the cost of setting up a living trust to be more than the cost of preparing a will. Remember, however, that the real cost of a will also includes the cost of probate. You will pay more initially, but in the long run a living trust will save you and your family money.

Most people should be able to get a living trust prepared for somewhere between $700.00 and $1000.00. Costs can be higher or lower, depending on how complex your plan is, where you live, who handles the property retitling (you or the attorney), if you need additional tax planning, etc. Prices are getting more competitive as living trusts become more popular. Most living trust attorneys offer "flat rate" trust pricing so you can find out the cost (and what it includes) up front, *before* you start your trust. It pays to shop around. Be suspicious of attorneys who won't give you a cost estimate. Also remember that setting up a living trust is usually a one-time cost. Once it is set up, it requires very little maintenance, most of which you can easily do yourself—for free.

You can help hold down the cost of your living trust. Remember, when you're talking with your attorney, you're "on the clock." You don't want to spend unnecessary time "chit-chatting" about living trusts and having him/her educate you about the general concept. Use your attorney's time and your money wisely: be specific with your questions as they relate to your individual situation. The more you know about living trusts and the more organized and prepared you are, the more you will save on attorney fees. Reading this book (or attending a living trust workshop) and completing the Information Form at the end of this book will help you make your decisions, get organized and minimize costs.

You can complete your part of setting up your living trust in just a few hours. After your initial attorney interview it should only take a couple of weeks for your attorney to prepare your living trust documents for you to review and approve. Allow another couple of weeks for your attorney to finalize your documents and for you to sign them.

No Special Government Forms Are Required

As long as one of the trust grantors is also an acting trustee, you continue to file the same personal income tax returns that you did before you set up your trust—the IRS does not require a separate income tax return for your living trust. And you do not need a separate tax identification number. You will continue to use your social security number.

Revocable

You can change or revoke your trust at any time. Trusts are very "user friendly" and easy to change. If, for example, you later decide to change your back-up trustee or disinherit one of your beneficiaries, then your attorney can prepare an *amendment* for a nominal cost. You don't need to have your entire trust redone or change the trust titling on your property. If you ever wanted to revoke your trust (although we can't imagine why you would do this) then just transfer all of your property back into your individual name. That's all there is to it.

Pre-Nuptial Agreement

A living trust can also serve as a very effective pre-nuptial agreement. Any property you put into your living trust *before you marry* remains the property of that trust, and stays separate from property accumulated *during* your marriage—even in community property states. If you die and your surviving spouse later remarries, a living trust could prevent him/her from being able to take your separate property into the new marriage. Just be careful not to contaminate your trust by combining your separate assets with your spouse's property.

These days, extended families are very common. If you have children from previous marriages, a living trust is an ideal way to make sure each child (and your new spouse) gets precisely what you intend for them to have—and nothing more. With a living trust, you can specify exactly what you want each to inherit and prevent the possibility of unintentionally disinheriting your children (as you could with joint ownership). You also reduce the chances that your wishes will be contested (as often happens with a will).

It is not uncommon for a family to have three living trusts. The spouses have a joint living trust for the property they have acquired *during* the marriage. Each spouse also has a separate living trust containing the property acquired *before* the marriage. The separate trusts distribute the property to each spouse's children (or other "blood relatives") from a previous marriage.

A Living Trust Can Reduce Estate Taxes

Married persons can use a living trust to reduce or eliminate estate taxes which could result in saving many thousands of dollars for your family. We'll explain how this is done in *Part Four*.

DOES A LIVING TRUST HAVE ANY DISADVANTAGES?

A properly prepared living trust does not have any *legal* disadvantages— it is a very traditional, well proven estate planning tool that has been used successfully for centuries. In fact, nothing else offers any greater legal protection for you and your family than a living trust. However, many attorneys and other professionals are not proficient in working with living trusts (or they have probate in mind for you). So there may be some misinformation about living trusts. This usually occurs as a result of not understanding how a trust actually works. Let's examine some of the "disadvantages" and objections to living trusts and clear up some of that misinformation.

A Living Trust Costs More Than A Will

Not really. Initially a living trust will probably cost more than a will, but the trust completely avoids probate. The true cost of a will includes the costs of probate, so when you fairly compare "apples with apples," a living trust is actually much less expensive than a will.

A Living Trust Is Complicated And Involves A Lot Of Paperwork

It does take a little time and effort on your part to retitle your assets and change your beneficiary designations. But since living trusts have become so popular, most businesses and government agencies have developed their own forms and procedures to efficiently handle retitling. Using an experienced living trust attorney can really streamline the process and provide back-up assistance if you need help. Once you set up your living trust and retitle your property into your trust name, you will continue to manage your affairs just as you did before.

A Living Trust Makes Refinancing Real Estate Difficult

As we explained earlier, lenders are often reluctant to refinance real estate titled in a living trust name. The easiest way to solve this problem is to *temporarily* deed the property back to yourself as an *individual,* complete the loan transaction, and then deed the property back to your trust. Just make sure you sign both deeds at the same time in case you become incapacitated or die *before* the refinancing is completed. Your back-up trustee can record the second deed putting your home back into your trust to keep it out of probate. Refinancing can be handled easily by using standardized quit claim deed forms; your attorney should be able to provide blank forms to your lender or title company. The cost will be nominal, usually just the deed recording fees.

And remember that federal regulations now allow lenders to make residential loans *directly* to a living trust. Ask the mortgage company if they will make the loan to your trust before you start your loan application. It's a good idea to shop around to find a company who will lend directly to your trust.

Setting Up A Living Trust Requires A Bank To Be Involved

Absolutely not. Trust law allows your living trust to be managed by you and your spouse acting as trustees with your selected family members as back-up trustees. So it's your choice whether or not to have a corporate trustee involved in your living trust. And since *you* (as trustee of your trust) cannot charge a fee to yourself (as grantor), you will *not* have any annual trustee's fee or maintenance costs to pay when you choose to keep your trust a "family affair."

A Living Trust Doesn't Protect Me From Creditors And Lawsuits

Yes, this is true. The legal purpose of a living trust estate plan is to avoid probate and save estate taxes. A living trust doesn't protect you from creditors and lawsuits because it doesn't change your situation or responsibilities. As a practical matter most people pay their bills and carry insurance for lawsuit protection so this is not a problem.

No Time Limit On Creditor's Claims

The probate process restricts the length of time creditors have to file claims (and lawsuits such as a will contest) against your estate. Once this time period (also called a "statute of limitations") has passed, no new claims can be presented.

Most state laws do not provide for a living trust "claims period" so a claim or lawsuit could be filed against your beneficiaries after the trust assets have been distributed. The statute of limitations period would vary from state to state depending upon the kind of property and the type of claim or lawsuit. However, because it is an extremely difficult and expensive process to sue the beneficiaries of a living trust, this risk is very remote.

Several states have recently passed laws giving living trusts the same claim period for creditors' claims as in probate. These laws will eventually spread to every state due to the increasing popularity of living trusts, which will completely eliminate this minor risk.

Some attorneys will advise you to deliberately leave one asset out of your trust to be probated at your death. If any claims are presented, then your back-up trustee can transfer just enough assets from your trust to pay the claim. All the rest of your assets are protected from probate by your trust, and claims are then limited to the probate claims period.

We do not recommend that you do this. Why go out of your way to attract attention, especially if it exposes your estate to frivolous claims or nuisance lawsuits. Remember, too, that your pour over will (we'll discuss this more in **Part Three**) will have to be filed with the court. Because it "pours over" any assets passing under the will into your living trust, you run the risk of the probate judge ordering your trust document to be produced for the court file. This means that your private family trust plan will become a public record. Keep the "business leverage" on your side by forcing creditors to deal directly with your back-up trustee or beneficiaries outside of the probate court.

Bankruptcy

You *may* lose some of your bankruptcy protection if certain assets, such as your home, are in your living trust name. This depends upon what state you live in. Of course, you can take your home out of trust *before* you file the bankruptcy to restore full protection and eliminate this alleged trust disadvantage.

Homestead Allowance

Some states reduce real estate taxes for *individually* owned homes; this is usually called a "homestead allowance." States may have other allowances such as Veteran's, over sixty-five, blind, disabled, etc. Homes titled in trust name usually qualify for the allowance, but your attorney should advise you if there is a problem and tell you what to do so that your home will still be protected by your trust and remain eligible for the allowance.

In summary, the "disadvantages" we have just discussed should not affect your decision to set up a living trust estate plan. Most of them affect very few people. At worst, they may result in some minor inconvenience, which is far outweighed by the many advantages a living trust provides.

WHY AREN'T LIVING TRUSTS BETTER KNOWN?

If living trusts are so wonderful, why don't we hear as much about them as we do about wills?

First of all, because the legal profession has become very specialized, many attorneys don't know that much about living trusts. But wills are so common that practically every attorney feels he/she can prepare one. It's easier for them to draw up a standard will—especially when that's what most people ask for—than to take the extra time to learn about something that isn't their specialty. It also takes time to educate a client. So, like most of us, they stick with what they (and their clients) know.

Secondly, the legal profession has become very competitive and many attorneys don't want to risk losing a client. Rather than refer a client to another attorney who specializes in living trusts, they may not bring up the subject. So, unless you specifically ask about a living trust, your attorney may not take the initiative to tell you about something he/she doesn't do.

Third, as in all professions, there are those who don't think of your best interests first. These attorneys earn a substantial part of their living from the probate system. They are more than happy to draft your will for a nominal charge while you are living, because they have an excellent chance of probating your will when you die. In fact, some may encourage you to name them as the attorney to represent your estate in probate. This is called "building a will file." Attorneys like this just wait for you to die so they can collect legal fees from your estate when it goes through probate.

And if you become incapacitated or leave minor children, they will probably represent you or your children in a probate conservatorship or guardianship, which can also be a very lucrative source of attorney fees. Remember, one of the biggest expenses of probate is attorney fees, which can quickly add up to many thousands of dollars. Not too many of these attorneys are anxious to offer living trusts, simply because living trusts avoid probate and would cut off a substantial source of future income for these attorneys.

But don't give up and try to do this yourself. You *need* a competent attorney, and there are many "top notch" estate planning lawyers who know about living trusts, believe in them, and do them all the time. In fact, more and more people are finding out about living trusts and, in response to the public's growing awareness and demand for them, there are some attorneys and law firms who now specialize in living trust estate planning.

These attorneys feel a moral and ethical responsibility to educate their clients about living trusts as an alternative to probate. This is the kind of attorney you want to advise you and help you to set up yours. In **Part Three** we'll give you information to help you find one of these attorneys.

COMPARISON AT A GLANCE

	With No Will	With A Will	With A Living Trust
If you Become Incapacitated	**Probate.** Court appoints conservator/guardian who reports to court; court controls your finances and assets and approves all bills.	**Probate.** Same as with no will.	**No probate.** Your back-up trustee manages your financial affairs according to your instructions for as long as necessary.
Court Costs and Attorney Fees	All court costs and attorney fees are paid from your assets.	Same as with no will.	None.
At Your Death	**Probate.** Court orders your debts paid and your possessions distributed according to state law.	**Probate.** After verifying your will, court orders your debts paid and your possessions distributed according to your will.	**No probate.** Your back-up trustee pays your bills and immediately distributes your possessions to your beneficiaries according to your instructions.
Court Costs and Attorney Fees	Your estate pays all court costs and attorney fees (estimated at 5% to 10% of your estate's gross value).	Same as with no will. If your will is contested, costs will be higher.	None.

	With No Will	With A Will	With A Living Trust
Time	Usually 1-2 years or longer.	Same as with no will.	Smaller estates usually 4-6 weeks, larger estates somewhat longer.
Flexibility and Control	**None.** Your property is controlled and distributed by probate court according to state law. Anyone can make a claim to your estate.	**Limited.** You can change your will at any time, but it can easily be contested. Your family has no control over probate costs or delays.	**Total.** You can change your trust at any time, even discontinue it. Your property remains under the control of your trust. Very difficult to contest.
Privacy	**None.** Probate proceedings are public record. Exposes your family to exploitation by unscrupulous and greedy relatives, salespersons, and scam artists.	**None.** Same as with no will.	**Total.** Privacy preserved. No probate. Living trusts are not public record.
Minor Child	**Probate.** Court takes control of the inheritance and appoints guardian. All decisions and financial transactions require court approval. Child receives funds at legal age (18 in most states).	**Same as with no will.** Children's trust in a will provides limited protection, but the will must be probated first and cannot go into effect if you become incapacitated.	**No probate.** Your appointed trustee manages the child's assets and provides funds for your child's medical care, education, support, etc., according to your instructions until your child reaches the age you specify. Court must approve guardian, but cannot overrule your choice of trustee and has no control over the child's inheritance.
Court Costs and Attorney Fees	All court costs and attorney fees are paid from your child's inheritance.	Same as with no will.	None.

Now that we've introduced you to the living trust concept, we want to help you get a living trust of your own. In this section we will discuss some of the things you'll need to think about, give you the additional information you need to make educated decisions, explain some terms you will need to know, and help you find the right attorney to do the legal paperwork.

In the back of this book is a tear-out Information Form that will help you organize your personal information and write down your decisions. Take the completed Information Form with you when you go to meet with your attorney. You'll probably still have some questions to ask about your individual situation, but you'll save time and money by being prepared.

YOU MUST MAKE SOME BASIC DECISIONS

First you need to think about what you want to happen if you become incapacitated and when you die. Your attorney will then put your instructions into your living trust document. These decisions include:

Δ   Who do you want to take care of you and manage your financial affairs if you become incapacitated?

Δ   If you become incapacitated, then do you have specific requests about your medical care?

Δ   Who do you want to *distribute* your property when you die?

Δ   Who do you want to *receive* your property and personal belongings?

Δ   If you have minor children, then who do you want to manage their inheritance if you and/or your spouse become incapacitated or die?

Δ   Who do you want to raise your children if you are unable to?

Δ   When do you want your children to receive their inheritance?

Δ   Do you have a child, grandchild, spouse, parent or family member with special needs or requiring special care?

Δ   If there are stepchildren in your family, what, if anything, do you want them to inherit?

Δ   Are there any persons you want to disinherit?

Δ   Do you want to leave something to your church or favorite charity?

Δ   If your entire family dies with or before you, then who would you want to receive your property?

Δ   If you have pets, then who do you want to take care of them?

You may also have special instructions you want in your trust. For example, if you become incapacitated and your trustee needs money to pay your medical expenses, then you may prefer that a certain piece of property be sold before others. You might want to pre-select the physician(s) who will determine if you are incapacitated and unable to manage your affairs. Perhaps you want the trust fund for your special needs child to be invested only in securities issued and guaranteed by the United States government. You will probably think of other special instructions—just put them on your Information Form and discuss them with your attorney. He/she will know if the information should be included in your living trust or in a separate letter to your back-up trustees and family.

Who Will Be Your Trustee?

As we said earlier, you will probably want to be your own trustee. If you are married, then you and your spouse will probably be co-trustees. You will continue to handle your personal and financial affairs just like you always have. But you can also name someone else as your trustee if you don't feel capable or, if for some reason, you just don't want to manage your own affairs anymore. You can always change your mind later and become your own trustee.

Another option is to name someone, such as a trusted son or daughter, to be a co-trustee with you. You, as the trust owner, still have control and you can replace your co-trustee at any time. If something happens to you, then your co-trustee can assume control immediately because he/she is already authorized to transact business on your trust. Understand, too, that a co-trustee is much different from a joint co-owner. Your co-trustee is legally required to follow your trust instructions and, because they are technically acting in the capacity of trustee and not individually, you and your assets are not liable should your co-trustee have bankruptcy or lawsuit problems.

Who Do You Want As Your Back Up Trustees?

Selecting your back-up trustees is one of the most important decisions you will make. Remember, your back-up trustee will take control for you if you (and your co-trustee) become incapacitated. When you die, your back-up acts just like an executor—paying your final bills, preparing and filing your final tax returns and distributing your property according to the instructions in your trust. Back-up trustees have a lot of power and responsibility, so choose them very carefully. Don't select anyone you wouldn't trust with your life. And remember that your back-up trustee cannot change your written plan. A back-up trustee's responsibility as your fiduciary is to follow your instructions.

Although most back-up trustees are adult children or family members, the old saying "blood is thicker than water" is not always what is best for you. For instance, naming your forty-year-old alcoholic son as your back-up trustee is probably a one-way street to disaster, especially if *you* become incapacitated and leave him in control of your assets. Be *realistic* and protect yourself by naming someone more trustworthy.

You should name several back-up trustees just in case the first is unable or unwilling to serve for any reason. They should be people you know and trust, demonstrate judgment you respect, and you should be able to trust that they will respect your wishes. They do not have to live in the same state you do, and they do not have to be members of your family.

If you have adult children, then they can be named as back-up trustees. If you wish, you can name two or more back-up trustees to share the responsibilities (you may, for instance, want two of your adult children to act together). You should also consider an impartial back-up, such as another family member, a trusted friend or a corporate trustee, to prevent any deadlocks or major disagreements. This doesn't mean you have "bad" children, but "honest men and women can honestly disagree." If your two children are in agreement, then the third co-trustee cannot overrule their decisions. But if they disagree, the third co-trustee can look at the situation from an objective and unemotional point of view and side with the trustee who has the most sensible suggestion—in effect acting as a "tie-breaker." We don't recommend more than three though— you don't want your affairs being run by a committee.

For some reason, parents tend to list their children as back-ups in order of birth, as if being older makes one more capable. You should list them in order of your choice starting with who you think will do the best job for you. However, children are very sensitive about these things and may get their feelings hurt if they aren't named at all. We generally suggest that you list all of your children as back-ups, but in order of your preference.

A back-up trustee should be trustworthy, have a sense of fair play, be able to make decisions on a rational and logical basis, and want this responsibility. It is a good idea (and a common courtesy) to ask the people you are considering if they want the responsibility. Reviewing the *Instructions for Back-Up Trustees* at the end of this section will help you and your back-ups understand what their duties and responsibilities will be.

Checks On Your Back-up Trustee

A living trust gives a lot of power to your back-up trustee. But a properly prepared trust will require that when your back-up trustee becomes your acting trustee, he/she must keep all of your other back-ups informed of all actions. This ensures that the trustee can be monitored.

In addition, a trust is a binding legal contract (unlike a will, which is simply a statement of your wishes and is only effective at death). Trustees are *fiduciaries,* so by law they have a legal responsibility to follow your trust instructions and act in a prudent (conservative) manner at all times. Obviously your back-up trustee should be someone you can trust but, as a safeguard, if your acting trustee were to "abuse" his/her fiduciary duties (by failing to follow the instructions in your trust document), then he/she could be removed as trustee and held personally liable.

Your acting trustee has broad powers to manage your trust, but he/she always has the legal obligation to carry out your instructions. This is very different from just giving someone a general "power of attorney" (often used in do-it-yourself kits and form books), which gives that person total freedom to legally sign your name with no plan or instructions to follow.

In any case, if you have any doubts about your back-up trustees' abilities to make decisions for you, if you're not sure about their business sense, or if you think they may act emotionally rather than logically and rationally, then you should probably select someone else or a bank as your back-up trustee.

You will probably want to be your own trustee

Should I Name A Corporate Trustee?

Corporate trustees are appointed back-up trustees because they are usually equipped to handle trust services economically and efficiently. They can manage your investments according to your instructions, handle all of the accounting, prepare trust tax returns, distribute income, and distribute the assets to your beneficiaries when you die. Some people have no family or friends they can trust, so they use a corporate trustee for maximum protection. A corporate trustee is sometimes preferred because family members are too emotionally involved to make sound decisions. And sometimes a corporate trustee is named as back-up as an alternative to offending the family members who were not asked to be one. A corporate trustee also offers long term continuity—they don't become incapacitated, die or move away, so you have the assurance that your trust will be managed for today and tomorrow.

Corporate trustees are very familiar with living trusts and will be more than happy to discuss them with you. Be sure to ask how long they have been in business, how many trusts they manage, what is the total value of the assets under their management, what services do they offer, what types of assets will they accept (or not accept), what types of reports do they make, etc. Corporate trustees are generally dependable, can act unemotionally and are convenient (especially banks, since most people bank near home). Corporate trust departments are also strictly regulated by federal and state agencies and they are insured and bonded.

Fees

Trustees are entitled to receive a reasonable fee for their services and, while family members seldom charge, a corporate trustee will begin charging a trustee fee as soon as it starts to *act*. If you are considering naming a corporate trustee as your back-up, then ask for a fee schedule so you will know what it charges. The schedule should thoroughly explain total fees, including termination fees, fees for extra statements, "base fees," tax preparation fees, incidental charges, etc. Most corporate trustees also have minimum requirements on the size of trust they will accept. At some, the minimum size is as low as $50,000 to $100,000. Many people have that much in life insurance alone. Depending on your relationship with your corporate trustee and the amount and type of assets you have, the fee and minimum requirements are often negotiable—check with your trust officer.

Most people think of a bank trust department when they hear the term *corporate trustee*, but this term also includes brokerage company trust departments and regulated trust companies, which offer trust services only. Trust management has become very competitive. You have many options, so it's wise to shop around for the company that best fits your needs.

Corporate trustees are most often used when the estate is large and complex, when the estate plan will continue for a long time, or when the person setting up the estate plan has no family or no family he/she can trust. Corporate trustees definitely have their place, but they are not for everyone. Most living trust estate plans are set up with you (and your spouse) as trustees and with family members as your back-ups.

Disadvantages of A Corporate Trustee

A corporate trustee will begin charging a fee as soon as they start acting. By naming *yourself* as trustee to manage your trust, the fees are avoided. And since most family member back-ups do not charge, it's more cost effective not to use a corporate trustee.

Corporate trustees tend to be impersonal, inflexible, and not good at making human decisions. For example, don't expect your trust officer to check on you in the nursing home. They also prefer to manage liquid assets such as cash, stocks, bonds, and treasury bills. Corporate trustees usually sell non-liquid assets such as homes, farms, antiques, heirlooms, etc., or they may *refuse* to accept a particular asset which means it will have to be probated (unless your trust has provisions to prevent this from happening). You should thoroughly check out the investment philosophy of your corporate trustee—otherwise those rental properties you so carefully acquired and managed over the years and planned to leave to your grandchildren may instead be put on the auction block and sold when you die.

Corporate trustees like to emphasize their *professional* investment experience, but this can only be verified by checking to see what their actual investment performance has been over the years. There is no evidence to prove that corporate trustees manage assets any better, or any worse, than other institutions (mutual funds, etc.) or individuals. You need to carefully check the facts first.

Realize that your corporate trustee will change over time. You have no assurance that the trust officer you deal with today will be there when the time comes to handle your trust. Investment policies sometimes change, especially if your corporate trustee merges or is bought out by another institution. It is important that you plan ahead and build extra protection into your trust if your corporate trustee changes.

Corporate trustees have a reputation for being overly conservative, slow, expensive and bureaucratic. While some certainly do fit this profile, many do not. Consider a corporate trustee who actively solicits and welcomes your business. The best corporate trustee is customer friendly, offers competitive rates and efficient services, is conservative and reliable. Corporate trustees, like people, are all different so it makes sense to shop around and find the one that can best handle your needs.

Don't Give Your Corporate Trustee A "Golden Parachute"

Some trusts continue for a long time after the grantor's death and much can happen during that time. Your corporate trustee may change investment philosophy, be acquired by another institution, raise its trustee fees unreasonably, or have no interest in responding to your beneficiary's needs beyond the absolute minimum required. Your beneficiaries may relocate, making it more convenient (and less expensive) to have a local corporate trustee.

In many living trusts the corporate trustee is guaranteed the position (and the fees) until the trust ends. By not planning ahead you have handed them a *golden parachute* in the form of a permanent job, which is probably not what you wanted. We recommend that your trust include provisions to give your beneficiaries (or your individual back-up co-trustees while acting with a corporate co-trustee) the option to replace your corporate trustee with another one. This option usually allows a corporate trustee to be replaced annually, but your trust could provide for a different time. The r*eplacement* corporate trustee should have the same amount of trust assets under management and employ the same number of trust officials as your initial choice.

With this arrangement, your corporate trustee has a real business incentive to be responsive to the needs of your beneficiaries to avoid being replaced as trustee. This also gives your family flexibility if circumstances should change. By establishing minimum requirements for the replacement trustee you ensure that the standards of the corporate trustee you originally selected (size, number of trust officials, etc.) will be maintained until your trust ends.

Don't forget: if you have minor children, then your living trust should include a children's trust to prevent the probate court from taking control of their inheritance.

Selecting A Guardian

If you have minor children, then you will need to select a guardian for them. This is a very important decision. The person you name will be responsible for raising your children if both their parents are dead or incapacitated. Guardians must be adults. You will, of course, want to choose someone who respects your values and standards (moral, ethical and religious) and will raise your children the way you would.

Being a guardian and raising someone else's children is a big responsibility, so make sure you thoroughly discuss this with your guardian choices and get their approval in advance. You should also name a back-up just in case your first choice is unable or unwilling to act. If you select a married couple, then you should specify which spouse you select to continue as your children's guardian if the couple divorces. And you can name successor guardians if you don't want your children to be raised in a single-parent family.

As we explained earlier, the court must still approve your selection, but it usually accepts your choice. Remember that the other natural parent is always the court's preferred choice. If you are a single parent with custody and really don't want your "ex" to be guardian, then go ahead and name your preference. It's possible that your "ex" may not be able to take the responsibility or won't want it. And the court may agree that your "ex" is not a suitable choice and would want to know your choice as an alternative.

Your Children's Trustee

Remember, the guardian is only responsible for *raising* your children and does not control the children's inheritance. You need to name a trustee for your children's trust—someone who will be responsible for the safekeeping of their inheritance and will wisely allocate the money for education, medical care, maintenance and other needs from the assets in the children's trust.

Most parents name the same person as trustee and guardian, making it convenient for one person to take care of their children. However, a children's trustee can be another individual, a corporate trustee or, if you wish, you can name co-trustees.

Children's trusts are not all alike. You should select the trust which best fits *your* situation. For example, if your children are all about the same age you will probably want a "share trust." Your children's trust subdivides into a share (also called a "sub-trust") for *each* of your children. Each child's financial needs are then handled from his/her *separate* trust share.

There might be a large gap between the ages of your children. The younger child's financial needs will last longer than the older child's. This means that a younger child's trust share could be used up *before* he/she even finished high school while an older child might be able to finish college and still have money left over. To avoid this situation, you can use a "pot trust" (also called a "sprinkle trust"). All of the children's trust assets remain in one trust and your trustee, at his/her discretion, can "sprinkle" the trust assets to provide for each child's individual needs as they grow up. When the youngest child reaches a pre-set age, the pot trust typically ends by distributing an equal share of the remaining assets to each child. The pot trust could also convert into a share trust and continue with a separate share for each child. So you see, you have a great deal of flexibility in how to set up the children's trust to best tailor it to your own situation.

Age Of Distribution

Your children's trust will specify when each child is to receive his/her trust share (called the "age of distribution"). Instead of giving the inheritance to a child when he/she becomes an adult (age eighteen in most states), you may want to keep "strings" on the children's inheritance until each child reaches an age at which you feel he/she will be mature enough to have outright control, such as age 21 or 25. "Stair stepping"— distributing the child's inheritance in *installments*—is becoming very popular. For example, you can specify a predetermined amount at certain ages—half of the inheritance at age twenty-three and the remainder at age twenty-five, spreading the payments out rather than one lump sum. It's completely up to you. You just need to specify how long you want the trustee to keep control.

You also have the option of continuing your children's trust for the *lifetime* of the child. This may be necessary if, for example, one of your children is irresponsible or has a chronic problem with alcohol, drugs, or gambling. The trustee manages and invests the inheritance and provides for the child's needs as they arise. When the child dies, the remaining assets in the children's trust are typically distributed to his/her children (your grandchildren).

If You Have A Disabled (Special Needs) Child

If you have a child with special needs (mentally or physically disabled as a result of birth defects, injury, alcohol or drug abuse), then your living trust should include a "special needs trust" (also called a "supplemental trust") so that the disabled child can continue receiving governmental benefits to which he/she may be entitled. In this situation, after your death the trust fund will *supplement*—but not *replace*—government benefits that your child receives. The child continues to receive benefits because the trust fund is not owned by him/her. Your trust will provide for the disabled child's needs above and beyond what the government will pay for.

Usually a close family member (brother, sister, etc.) is named as trustee for the disabled child. This could create a conflict of interest if the trustee will inherit from the trust when the disabled child dies—the priority might shift from providing adequately for the disabled child to preserving the trust assets for their own use. In that situation a corporate trustee (or a family member and a corporate trustee as co-trustees) might be a better choice.

A special needs trust is actually a special kind of children's trust. A regular children's trust won't work. It must be properly worded, or the government can disallow the child's benefits until all of the assets in the special needs trust have been depleted.

It can also be used for any disabled dependents. You can fund it with all or just a portion of your estate. The amount depends upon the child's age, life expectancy, type of disability, level of care required, size of your estate, and whether or not you want to include other beneficiaries. When the disabled child dies, the assets remaining in the supplemental trust are usually distributed to his/her children or to your other children.

It's very important that you know about a special needs trust if you have a disabled child. And it is also important that you know that it is, at best, limited protection. Congress is always rewriting the laws in this area so it's possible that it will restrict or even take away the special needs trust. Make certain that you use an experienced attorney to prepare and periodically review your special needs trust to ensure that you provide maximum protection for the disabled child.

SELECTING YOUR BENEFICIARIES

Your beneficiaries are the persons and/or organizations you select to receive your property and possessions when you die. Most people prefer to pass their property down through their bloodline, but you can leave it to any person or organization you wish. There are some things you need to consider as you decide when and how you want your beneficiaries to receive their inheritances. In the following pages we'll explain some of your choices.

Per Capita Or Per Stirpes Distribution?

Children sometimes die *before* their parents. If this happened in your family, then how would you want your surviving children to inherit? You have two options—distribution by "per capita" or "per stirpes" (pronounced "per stir peas"). These old legal terms can be confusing, but the following examples will help you to understand how they work.

Per Capita: This means that only the children who are *surviving* at your death will inherit your estate—the descendants of a predeceased child (your grandchildren) will not receive anything. For example: Mary, a widow, has three adult children, Louis, Cindy and John. John dies leaving two children—Jennifer and Lauren (Mary's grandchildren). Then Mary dies. Her trust distributes Mary's estate in equal shares to her children, *per capita*. This means Louis and Cindy would equally share *all* of Mary's estate. Mary's grandchildren by John would not receive anything—they were disinherited because John died before his mother.

EXAMPLE OF PER CAPITA DISTRIBUTION

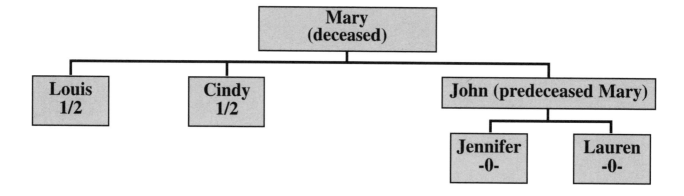

Per Stirpes: Under this option the descendants of a deceased child will equally inherit the share of their deceased parent. Let's use the same family, except in this example assume Mary's trust distributes her estate equally to her children, *per stirpes.* Her estate is now divided into three equal shares. One third goes to Louis, one-third to Cindy, and one-third to John—but since John died before Mary, his share is given to his children equally, with Jennifer and Lauren each receiving a one-sixth share. *Per stirpes* allows your estate to flow through a deceased child to your descendants by that child.

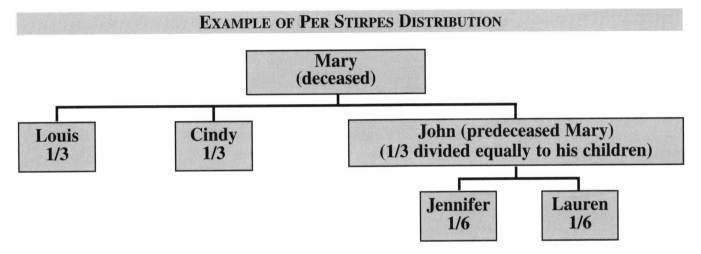

EXAMPLE OF PER STIRPES DISTRIBUTION

Although most people prefer per stirpes, the choice is yours. Just make sure your trust clearly states what you want.

You may be interested to know that most people specify a per capita distribution for their personal property and effects. Children are usually very emotional and sentimental about a deceased parent's personal belongings, so most parents feel it's best to leave their personal property to their children only. Parents usually prefer the remaining estate (also called the "residuary estate") to be distributed per stirpes, so they don't risk disinheriting grandchildren by a deceased child.

There is no right or wrong distribution plan. Once you understand your options, select the one that you feel is best for your family.

Distribution By Dollar Amounts Or Percentages?

Distributions by percentages are almost always better than a specific dollar amount distribution, because you don't know what your estate's value will be when you die. To illustrate, let's assume your estate is $200,000, and you decide to leave $50,000 to your church and everything else to your only son. When you die your estate has shrunk to $90,000, which means your church still gets $50,000, but your son receives only $40,000. This is not at all what you intended.

If your instructions had instead distributed 25% of your estate to your church and 75% to your son, then 25% of $90,000 or $22,500 would go to your church, and 75% of $90,000 or $67,500 would go to your son. A percentage distribution is far more flexible and preserves your original plan whether or not your estate later increases or decreases in value.

Giving To Charities, Churches And Foundations

This is an excellent time to think about giving to a favorite charity or foundation. Take a few minutes to think about organizations or causes that are special to you—some national, perhaps international, and some local. Many are excellent, and they are all in need of funding to continue their work. There is sure to be one or more that you would like to help. In addition to the tax benefits of charitable donations, you have the power to do something good, to express yourself, and to put something of value back into the world.

For example, you may have been very active in your church, synagogue, or other religious or charitable organization. Perhaps one has provided support to you at a critical time in your life, and you would like to return the support. Maybe someone very close to you has died from cancer, alzheimer's disease, AIDS or some other disease, and you would like to help fund research to find a cure. Many people give in the memory of a loved one. You may feel very strongly about education, the hungry and homeless, protecting the environment, world peace, animal rights, the arts, organ donation—the list of worthwhile causes is endless.

Your gift can be as specific or as general, as large or as small, as you want to make it. You could set up a scholarship program for underprivileged children, buy new chairs or religious textbooks for your church or synagogue, or help fund a building project. The charity or foundation of your choice will be delighted to make suggestions and help you set up your gift program. Some may even be able to recommend an attorney who specializes in living trusts.

Most organizations feel they have a moral obligation to protect and look after the welfare of their members—a "we take care of our own" philosophy. Educating their members about the living trust alternative to probate is consistent with this responsibility. If your organization does

100%

of your

gift

will

go to

the charity

or

foundation

not know about living trusts, or endorses a program that relies on using only a will, you may want to lend them your copy of this book.

Giving is very easy with a living trust

Just make your instructions clear by specifying the exact name and address of the organization you want to receive your gift. Include the amount of the gift (remember percentages are better than fixed dollar amounts) and whether the gift is *unrestricted*, meaning the organization can decide how to use the gift, or *restricted*, which limits the gift to a specific purpose. If the gift is to be restricted, make sure you clearly describe how it is to be used.

Just in case your organization doesn't exist when you die, you should probably name an alternative choice. With a living trust you can be sure your wishes are carried out—unlike a will, which is often contested by the heirs to prevent charitable donations. And because there are no probate costs or delays, 100% of your gift will immediately go to the charity or foundation of your choice.

Grandchildren

You have the option of splitting your estate between your children and your grandchildren. You can also leave your entire estate to your grandchildren. The choice is yours. Just don't risk a probate guardianship by leaving assets *directly* to your *minor* grandchildren. You don't have to set up a separate trust to do this. A children's trust (for your grandchildren) can be included inside your living trust. This allows you to specify *how* and *when* you want your grandchildren to receive their inheritance.

Stepchildren

If there are stepchildren in your family, then you must decide if you want them to inherit from you. The subject of stepchildren can be very touchy, but you and your spouse need to talk about this openly and honestly. Your living trust plan should clearly outline how your estate will be shared by your children and stepchildren when you die—and when your spouse dies.

Disinheriting

Are there any family members that you specifically want to exclude?

Sometimes there are very good reasons to disinherit someone. Although it can be a very emotional decision, if this is something that is important to you, then it should be included in your living trust estate plan.

Alternate Beneficiaries

You should also consider who you would want your property to go to if all of the people you have named as your beneficiaries die before you. Many people specify more distant relatives, close friends, their church, a favorite charity, or foundation.

Special Gifts

You may want to leave specific items to certain individuals, like a favorite piece of jewelry or an antique that you want a special friend or relative to have. These are called "special gifts" or "special bequests." With a living trust, this is very simple. All you need to do is make a separate list of the items you want to give to specific people or organizations (including your titled property). You date and sign the list, have it notarized, and keep it with your living trust document. Your attorney should provide you with the special gifts forms and instructions. If you later change your mind, then just destroy the old list and make a new one. You don't have to change your trust document. You can do it at home—just make sure you destroy the old list and have the new list signed, dated and notarized. The new list is a legally recognized *amendment* to your living trust, so you can make changes any time you want.

It's best to have a separate list for each person. To avoid confusion and family disagreements when you die, make the list as specific as you can. For example, the description "my gold watch" isn't much help if you own six gold watches when you die. "My gold watch with the initials JBD engraved on the back" is a much better description. It's much easier for you to do this yourself rather than for your children and other relatives to reach an agreement which satisfies everyone. If dissatisfaction occurs, these family disagreements could still prompt an estate sale.

With a will, changing your beneficiaries on anything other than your personal property is complicated and expensive. Most states permit you to make a separate list of your special gifts, but this is usually limited to your *personal* property (no cash or anything with titles). To specify who you want to receive your *titled* property (such as real estate, investments, bank accounts, etc.) or cash, the item must be specifically listed in your will, which is prepared by an attorney and witnessed. If you change your mind, then you have to go back to your attorney, and sign a will amendment (called a "codicil"). Of course, if you have a "do-it-yourself" will then you probably didn't use an attorney, and you may not have enough specific information to do this correctly to fulfill your state's requirements—and then you risk having both your special gifts list and your will ruled invalid by the court.

PUTTING EXTRA PROTECTION INTO YOUR LIVING TRUST

As we've said several times, all of your property should be included in your living trust to make it to work properly. You should change the titles on all of your titled property and beneficiary designations as soon as possible after your living trust document has been completed. However, something may happen to prevent you from changing all of them, or you may inadvertently forget one. For maximum protection (and convenience), we strongly urge that your living trust "estate plan" include the following.

Statement Of Your Intentions

First, there should be a special section in your living trust document stating that it is your *intention* that all of your property (titled and untitled, including your personal belongings and death proceeds from insurance policies, etc.) be included in your living trust, *unless you specifically exclude a certain property in writing*. It should also give your back-up trustee specific power to change the titles of any "forgotten" property to the name of your trust. This section should be separately signed and notarized, so it can be recorded if necessary.

This power should automatically extend to the back-up trustee who acts for you—it should go along with the trustee position, rather than being limited to a specific individual. This way, if your first choice for back-up trustee is unable to take over for you, your second choice (or third, if necessary) will have this authority. The instructions should be very specific—your back-up can only transfer titles and beneficiary designations to the name of your trust. This prevents your backup trustee from changing the titles of your property to someone other than your trust or from removing assets from your trust. You have already stated that you *intended* for all of your property to be in your trust—you are simply giving your backup trustee the power to carry out these instructions.

Make sure you change titles and beneficiaries to your trust

The intention, of course, is to make it impossible for anything you own to be subjected to probate. *We can't guarantee that this will work*—that decision will vary from court to court and will depend on the value and type of property or assets. But the legal theory is that your backup trustee could transfer titles after your death, and before probate proceedings can start. *This does not (and should never) take the place of changing titles and beneficiary designations when your trust is set up and as you accumulate additional property.*

Simple Pour Over Will—Another Safety Net

A properly prepared living trust plan includes a "simple pour over will," stating that anything you have inadvertently left out of your living trust will go into it at your death. This is an extra precaution in case the special paragraph discussed above is not accepted by the court. If this happens, then the "forgotten" property may have to be probated, but at least your simple pour over will "catches" the property and sends it back into your living trust. The property will then be distributed as part of your living trust plan.

Power Of Attorney—For Convenience

A durable power of attorney should always be included with a living trust. As we said earlier, a durable power of attorney ends at death, but will still be valid if you become incapacitated. We recommend you have a *durable* power, even if your state does not permit it. Remember, it is always better to have *too much* legal "horsepower" than not enough. You might be living in another state or own assets in another state at the time of your incapacity. A durable power of attorney can include special provisions for health care, which we will explain below.

Either type power of attorney (regular or durable) has a value when combined with your living trust. Your power of attorney should be given to the same people you name as your backup trustees (and co-trustee if you have one) and in the same order. This will allow the power of attorney to automatically transfer to the back-up who takes over for you, and it also keeps these special powers concentrated with just your back-up trustees.

We recommend that your durable power of attorney include a special provision giving your back-ups (in order of succession) not only the regular power to sign your name, but also the additional power to re-title any forgotten property from your name to the name of your trust. If you become incapacitated, and your back-up trustee discovers that you forgot to put a piece of property into your trust, then he/she should be able to change the title and put it into your trust for you.

We recommend inclusion of this provision in your durable power of attorney, even if your state does not recognize this arrangement. Your back-up trustee will not be able to use it if you are incapacitated, but if you are well and simply out of the country or otherwise unavailable, then your back-up can conveniently use it to re-title property and put it into your trust for you.

Your durable power of attorney should include a power of attorney for *health care*. This is mainly for convenience in making medical decisions. Although your living trust gives authority to your back-up trustee to act for you (or to your spouse if named as co-trustee), many medical institutions (such as hospitals and nursing homes) may not be completely familiar with living trusts. Rather than trying to educate them in an emergency, you can simply show them your power of attorney which is readily recognized by just about everyone. In these situations, a power of attorney is actually more appropriate than your living trust document. Besides, you will probably consider your living trust plan private, and you may not feel comfortable showing it to strangers.

These Are Only Extra Precautions

A properly prepared living trust is a powerful combination of three well-known and established legal tools—a living trust, a will and a power of attorney. Without all three your trust plan is defective and will not provide you with complete protection. But, in any event, these extra safety nets *do not* take the place of changing titles and beneficiary designations to your trust while you are alive and able. *Don't put off completing your trust* assuming that these provisions will do it for you. Failure to correctly re-title property will sabotage your living trust. Nothing can absolutely guarantee an assignment of all of your property to your trust if you don't change the titles and beneficiary designations.

Certificate of Trust

Some companies may insist upon having a *copy* of your trust document to be satisfied that you have a valid living trust. They want verification of your trust *before* they will change your titles. You may not want them to have access to your personal business and, because your trust is a private document, you have no legal obligation to give anyone a copy of your trust.

A properly prepared living trust includes a "certificate of trust" (also called a "trust abstract"). This is a short statement, signed by you and notarized, that contains only basic information about your trust such as the date it was signed, the names of the acting and back-up trustees, that it is a *revocable* trust, which state law it was set up under, etc. This certificate does not disclose any of your personal business, such as your beneficiaries.

A certificate of trust is very easy to use. You give a *copy* of the certificate to the company. It's convenient for them to file the certificate with your account information instead of filing copies of trust documents. Most companies now routinely accept certificates of trust, and many have developed their own certificate forms, which you sign when the account title is changed.

A few institutions, most notably title and abstract companies, still require a copy of the trust document for real estate transactions. To preserve your privacy, just remove the beneficiary provisions from the copy you give them. Make sure the company files your trust copy in the real estate *closing* file only. It should *never* be recorded.

A certificate of trust is an efficient way to show proof of your trust and maintain the privacy of your estate plan.

Consider A Health Care Directive

A "health care directive" (also called an "advance directive") is a document that states your instructions to your physician about your medical care if, for some reason, you are unable to make decisions for yourself. Health care directives include a "living will" (not to be confused with the living trust) and a durable power of attorney for health care—which we'll explain below.

Living Will

Living Wills have become very popular. President Nixon and Jacqueline Kennedy Onassis both had living wills. This is a document stating that you do *not* want extraordinary or "heroic" life support medical treatment if your physicians have certified that you are terminally ill or in a persistent vegetative ("brain dead") condition with no hope for recovery. More comprehensive living wills contain options that allow your instructions to be very specific about the procedures *you* want withheld or withdrawn, such as radiation, chemotherapy, mechanical ventilator, kidney dialysis, etc. A living will is only used when you are unable to give instructions about your medical treatment. You can revoke it at any time.

Stopping life support measures (other than those to relieve pain and to keep you comfortable) is a very personal decision. It can spare your family unnecessary emotional distress and allow you to "die with dignity" rather than maintaining a debatable quality of life that can last for years and be extremely expensive.

Durable Power of Attorney For Health Care

This document is more comprehensive than a living will. It is limited to medical care decisions. When combined with a living will, a durable power of attorney for health care is called a health care directive. It can also be a separate document or combined with a living will or included as a special provision in a durable power of attorney (for assets).

A durable power of attorney for health care lets you appoint *agents* who are legally authorized to make health care decisions for you (including enforcement of the provisions of your living will) if you are unable to make them yourself. This document can be very important if you ever need any type of surgery or medical treatment. You can revoke your health care power at any time. Your health care agents do not have to be the same persons as your back-up trustees. For example, you may want your business-minded son to be your back-up trustee, executor, and agent under your durable power of attorney (for assets); but you might prefer your daughter, the registered nurse, to be your health care agent.

We recommend that you have a durable power of attorney for health care even if it is not recognized in your state, because you might be hospitalized in a state that does recognize it.

Your attorney should include a health care directive when he/she sets up your trust. Otherwise most hospitals and care facilities can give you a health care directive form. Review it with your physician, and see how he/she feels about a health care directive—if they oppose it, then you should consider finding a doctor who does not oppose it. Make sure a copy of your directive is put in your patient file. Your health care agents should have a copy also.

HOW TO FIND THE RIGHT ATTORNEY TO SET UP YOUR LIVING TRUST

First of all, you have to find an attorney who believes in living trusts, preferably one who specializes in living trust estate planning. The best way to do this, of course, is through a personal referral from someone who has had a living trust prepared. Ask your family, friends, banker, broker, financial planner, church/synagogue, or charity to recommend an attorney who does living trusts. Get several recommendations and interview each attorney. You can shop by phone to screen out those who are too expensive, you don't think are qualified, or you just don't like. Avoid attorneys who won't talk to you by phone.

Questions you need to ask and things to keep in mind:

Δ   Ask the attorney how many living trust estate plans he/she has done. How much experience does the attorney have in this area and how long have they been doing living trusts? Does the attorney limit his/her practice to living trusts or do they practice in other types of law? If they do, then what other areas? How much malpractice insurance does the attorney have? This will give you a feel of how much importance the attorney places on living trusts.

Δ   Can the attorney provide you with any references, such as a bank, trust department, CPA? Ask if the attorney has written any books or articles on living trusts. You shouldn't pay to educate your attorney about living trusts. If the attorney has experience preparing living trust estate plans, then he or she will be much more efficient and knowledgeable. This will save you time and money. Plus, you will be confident that your living trust has been properly prepared.

Δ   Tell the attorney that you want a basic living trust estate plan that will keep your family out of probate when you die or if you become incapacitated. Be suspicious of an attorney who tries to talk you out of a living trust and wants to talk you into a will or joint ownership. Think again if the attorney tries to convince you that a living trust is complicated and expensive. Remember, most living trust documents are standardized and do not normally require much modification to take care of most people's needs.

Δ   Ask how the attorney charges for living trusts and what payment procedure he/she uses. Many attorneys charge by the hour, but those who specialize in living trusts will usually charge a flat rate fee. Ask the attorney for a living trust fee schedule.

We have included a copy of our fee schedule which you may find helpful in your search for the right attorney. Remember, you are looking for a good value for the fee you pay. Pricing will vary by geographical areas, by the level of attorney involvement (such as retitling your assets), and by whether the attorney uses flat rate or hourly fees. The following chart is just one example of the type of pricing you may find.

1996 AUSTIN LIVING TRUST FEE SCHEDULE

Simple Living Trust: Non-tax planning   **$790**
For the single person or husband and wife.
Estates under $600,000.

Tax Planning AB Trust   **$1,190**
For married couples.
Estates from $600,000 to $1.2 million.

Tax Planning BC Trust   **$1,190**
For the married person.
Separate estate greater than $600,000

Tax Planning ABC Trust   **$1,390**
For married couples.
Estates over $1.2 million.

The above fees include the following:

Unlimited free attorney consultations after trust is signed

2 individually customized Austin Living Trust documents

Pour-over Will

Durable Power of Attorney

Living Will

Certificate of Trust

Children's Trust and guardian provisions

Handicapped/Special Needs Trust

Health Care Power of Attorney

Special Gifts List Forms

Transfer letter forms and instructions

Simple quit claim deed to living trust (preparation only—for one real estate property)

Finding

the

right

attorney

is very

important

Briefly describe your situation and ask the attorney to give you a "ballpark" cost estimate in advance. Be sure to ask what the fee includes—trust document, durable power of attorney, pour-over will, certificate of trust, children's trust, etc. Keep in mind that if you need a tax planning living trust, or if your situation is complicated, you should expect to pay more.

Be suspicious of any attorney who is reluctant to talk about pricing. Don't be afraid or embarrassed to shop around and compare prices. But be realistic and don't trade price for quality. You want the best value, not the lowest cost.

Δ   You can learn a lot about the attorney by the way his/her phones are answered. Are your calls answered in a professional and courteous manner? Is the attorney accessible to take your call—if not, how long does it take for your call to be returned? A negative phone attitude and delays in returning calls are "red flags." Just think if your phone calls aren't promptly returned, your back-up trustee could be in a real predicament if there were an emergency and he/she needed to contact the attorney.

Δ   Where is the attorney located? You want to deal with someone who is convenient. Does he/she have evening office hours? Is the office open on weekends? You don't want to take time away from work if you don't have to.

Δ   Ask about the procedure and how long is required to complete your living trust estate plan. It should take no more than a few weeks to get everything done.

Δ   Can you come in for a free consultation? The attorney should be willing to spend 30-60 minutes with you—at no charge—to answer your general questions.

Δ   When you go in for your free consultation, look around the attorney's office. Is it neat and clean? Does the attorney appear to be well-organized?

Δ   Take this book and the Information Form with you and show it to the attorney. Be suspicious if the attorney tries to down-play the information and discourage you from wanting to stay out of probate. The attorney you want to deal with should endorse any information which correctly explains living trusts and helps you avoid probate.

Δ   Ask the attorney to show you samples of his/her basic living trust documents. Make sure the attorney has all of the necessary documents—living trust, durable power of attorney, pour-over will, certificate of trust, etc. (Use our fee schedule as a convenient checklist.) Where did the attorney get his/her trust documents? Are they produced from "off the shelf" generic trust software or did the attorney develop his/her own documents? Be suspicious of any attorney who doesn't have any documents or samples to show you or if he/she refuses to let you look at his/her basic trust documents.

Are the documents on a good quality paper with easy to read type? Do they present a well-organized appearance with headings, numbered paragraphs, etc. Trust documents should be letter-sized (8 1/2 x 11 inches) for convenient copying and filing.

Can you understand the documents? Remember trusts are legal documents so expect to find a lot of "legalese." Does the attorney include a written "plain English" explanation of the trust provisions?

Ask to see how the attorney packages his/her trust documents. Three ring binders may look impressive, but they aren't very practical, especially if you need to file additional papers (and don't have convenient access to a hole punch). Many attorneys use a vinyl "zipper portfolio bag" so you can conveniently file your papers just the way you want.

Δ   Does the attorney change your titles and beneficiary designations to your trust? (Is this an additional charge and if you later buy more property is there yet another fee?) Or does the attorney help you maintain control by teaching you how to do this yourself by providing you with the necessary forms and instructions? Experienced living trust attorneys will emphasize the importance of titling and have well-established procedures to make sure your assets are correctly put into your trust.

Δ   How much does it cost if you need to talk to the attorney after you set up your trust? This can become very expensive if you are charged every time you call with a question. You should know that many attorneys allow you unlimited telephone calls and office consultations to discuss general questions about your living trust. Some attorneys even provide a toll free number as an additional convenience to you. For certain, you will have questions from time to time so find out the cost (if any) in advance.

Living Trust Seminars

Due to the increasing popularity of living trusts, many attorneys now conduct free public seminars to explain living trusts. This is a good way to learn about living trusts in a group setting. It also gives you a chance to ask your questions (and listen to other people's questions) and "size-up" the attorney from a distance. Living trust seminars are usually advertised in local newspapers or by direct mail.

Look at the seminar hand-out materials. Are the hand-outs easy to understand and do they present a quality professional look?

Some attorneys sell books and tapes at seminars. Unless the item is also available at your local bookstore, *don't buy it*. It is probably not that good and most likely over-priced. Don't get distracted by sales pitches—the purpose of a seminar should be to present information and answer questions, not to sell products.

Was the presentation well organized and thorough? Were you able to understand it? Did the attorney give direct answers to the questions asked or was he/she evasive? Did the attorney explain how much he/she charges for a living trust? Some attorneys will give you a fee discount for attending the seminar which can be a benefit to you.

An excellent way to learn about living trusts is for you to attend several seminars. This lets you "compare and contrast" each presentation. Investing your time in learning (and shopping) up front can save you money and problems later on.

Think of a living trust as both a *product* and a *service*. You want the highest possible legal quality in your trust documents, so you need to find an experienced living trust attorney. You also want an attorney who is committed to servicing your trust, so that you are informed of any legal changes that might affect your trust later on, and so that the attorney will be available to answer your questions and handle your needs should your situation change. The *right* attorney will be dedicated to the quality of his/her work product and to servicing the client to the very best of his/her ability.

Personalities and confidence are very important. Your attorney should be someone with whom you are comfortable, someone to whom you can talk, and someone who seems to be genuinely interested in you and your family's welfare.

Does the attorney seem willing to answer all your questions, or do you feel that you are only taking up his/her time? Your attorney should encourage you to ask questions and voice your concerns.

Pre-Paid Legal Services Plans

One way to get your living trust done at a reasonable cost is through group or pre-paid legal services plans. These are becoming very popular and growing rapidly all across the country. Many employers, associations and unions offer them to their employees and members. Several are also offered directly to the public through credit cards. You should check to see if you qualify for membership in one—it could save you time and money on your living trust and on other legal matters.

Under these plans, some legal services such as review of legal documents and telephone or office consultations are free. (This is an ideal way to learn about their living trust services or to ask questions about your trust, at no cost, once it is set up.) Other services are offered at discounts, and there is usually a limit on the attorney's hourly rate. Some of these plans are national, so if you move to another state you can have your trust reviewed at little or no cost.

Most of these plans use local attorneys to provide the services. You will still need to personally interview attorneys until you find one who is experienced in living trust estate plans and with whom you feel comfortable. One of the oldest and best known national plans is *The Legal Services Plan, offered through* **The Signature Group.** *Its address is: The Legal Services Plan, 200 North Martingale Road, Schaumburg, IL 60173-2096. Or you can call 1-800-323-4620.*

You can also contact the American Prepaid Legal Services Institute and they can tell you which pre-paid plans are available in your state. *The American Bar Association is one of its supporters. The address is: The American Prepaid Legal Services Institute, 750 North Lake Shore Drive, Chicago, IL 60611.*

The Actual Process

Once you've found the right attorney for you, this is what should happen:

Δ   Take your completed Information Form and your written questions to your initial attorney interview. The attorney will review your information, discuss it with you, answer your questions and probably make some suggestions for you to consider. Make sure you get a definite cost from the attorney at this point—preferably in the form of a fee agreement signed by you and the attorney.

Δ   The attorney will prepare a draft of the living trust documents for you to review and approve. Make sure you read them carefully, and be sure you understand everything. Don't be afraid to ask questions.

Δ   After you have approved the draft, the final documents will be prepared for signing. This means you (and your spouse) will sign your living trust, and it will be notarized. There are usually two original documents—so that if you misplace one, you will still have another original. Your other documents, such as durable power of attorney, pour over will, certificate of trust, health care directive, and quit claim deeds, will be signed, witnessed and notarized at this time, too. After signing, your attorney should explain the trust titling procedures and give you detailed written instructions and the forms required to do this.

Δ   You then change the titles of all your property from your name to the name of your living trust. Don't forget to change beneficiary designations, too. You can do this yourself, dealing directly with your bank, savings and loan, credit union, employee benefits department, insurance agent, and broker. Your attorney does not have to do this for you, which means it will be less expensive. Just check with your attorney for the exact wording you should use on the titles.

Remember, your living trust estate plan is not complete until all titles and beneficiary designations have been properly changed to your trust name. It is your responsibility to make sure this happens.

INSTRUCTIONS FOR BACK-UP TRUSTEES

If you have been named a back-up trustee for someone, then you are probably wondering what you should do when that person dies or becomes incapacitated. Here is a brief checklist that will help give you direction at a time when you may not know where to begin.

At Death

Δ   Inform the family of your position and assist them as needed: funeral arrangements, flowers, cemetery marker, announcement in paper, special wishes for service, notifying friends, relatives, employer, etc.

Δ   Make sure you keep all back-up trustees fully informed throughout the process.

Δ   Order at least 6 certified death certificates (you can usually get these from the funeral home). You will generally need one for each company with whom the Grantor did business to transfer titles, etc. This will help speed things up, since you won't have to wait to get copies back in order to give them to someone else.

Δ   Stop monthly benefit payments such as Social Security, Veterans Administration, etc.

Δ   Notify the bank so you can start writing checks. The bank will probably want to see a certified death certificate (or an obituary), a copy of the trust document (or certificate of trust) and your personal identification.

Δ   Secure and inventory property, especially real estate. Make sure you have the only keys, keep the utilities on (or turn them off), keep homeowners insurance in force, etc. Remove valuables (jewelry, coin or stamp collections, works of art, stock certificates, etc.) and important documents to a safe place. Arrange for forwarding of mail. Start a list of all assets.

Δ   Assemble important papers, including the trust documents, real estate deeds, stock and bond certificates, insurance policies, bank books, automobile titles, etc.

Δ   Notify Social Security, Veterans Administration, life insurance companies, retirement plans, associations, and any others that will provide a death benefit. Put death proceeds in an interest bearing account until distributed.

Δ   Notify the attorney who prepared the trust document. He/she should be aware of the death in case you, beneficiaries or family members need to call with questions.

Δ   Collect any bills and start a ledger of accounts payable and income received.

Δ   Arrange to have real estate appraised (and any appreciated assets valued). Establish fair market value for all other assets.

Δ   Contact an accountant for preparation of final income tax return and estate/inheritance tax return (if applicable).

Δ   Check to see if any credit cards, installment loans, mortgage debts, etc., are covered by credit life insurance.

Δ   Make a list of all debts and claims against the estate.

Δ   Pay all bills and taxes.

Δ   Make a final accounting record of all assets, income received and bills paid. Give a copy to all back-up trustees and to the beneficiaries when the property is distributed.

Δ   Distribute property in this order (make sure you get a receipt signed by each beneficiary stating that he/she has received the final accounting and the property and releases you from your duties as trustee):

1. Property on special gifts lists, if any

2. Remaining personal property—hold estate sale if necessary

3. If children's trust, transfer property and cash to children's trustee

4. If no children's trust, divide cash and transfer titles of property according to trust instructions

Δ   Nothing else needs to be done—the trust has been dissolved.

At Incapacity

Δ   Check the trust document for specific instructions. Have the
appropriate physician write a letter documenting the person's
condition. Some trust documents will only require a letter from an
M.D., others from one or two specialists, etc.

Δ   Notify the bank and others that you are now the trustee for this
person. They will probably want to see a copy of the doctor's
letter, trust document (or certificate of trust) and your personal
identification.

Δ   Notify the attorney who prepared the trust document. He/she
should be aware of the incapacity in case you or family members
need to call with questions.

Δ   Secure and inventory any property, especially real estate. Make
sure you have the only keys and take care of any utilities, etc.
Remove valuables and important papers to a safe place. Arrange
for forwarding of mail.

Δ   Transact any necessary business for the incapacitated person. You
can apply for disability benefits, file tax returns, receive and
deposit funds, pay bills (including mortgage and other obligations)
and, in general, use the person's assets to take care of
him/her until recovery or death.

Δ   Keep a ledger of bills paid and any income received.

Δ   Make sure you keep all back-up trustees fully informed
at all times.

You know that a living trust completely avoids probate and all the costs that go along with it. It can also be used by married persons to reduce or eliminate estate taxes.

If the net value of your estate (the fair market value of all of your assets minus your debts) is more than $600,000 when you die, then federal estate taxes (death taxes) must be paid from your estate before it is distributed to your beneficiaries. If your estate is too small to be affected by this, then you can just skip over this chapter. But before you do, think for a moment: if you own a home or other real estate, then it could be worth a lot more than you think. Real estate can easily appreciate in value over the years and can continue to appreciate after you or your spouse die. You may have purchased additional life insurance or your investments may have appreciated substantially, increasing your estate. Because a tax-planning living trust can save your family thousands of dollars—in addition to the probate savings—you may want to continue reading.

Purpose

Revocable tax planning living trusts are used between married persons for the purpose of:

Δ   Avoiding probate at death or incapacity.

Δ   Providing for the surviving spouse.

Δ   Reducing or eliminating federal estate taxes on estates larger than $600,000.

Δ   Preventing a surviving spouse from completely changing or revoking the common trust plan following the death of his/her spouse.

Δ   Giving each spouse control over one-half of the assets in estates larger than $1.2 million.

Δ   Deferring estate taxes on estates larger than $1.2 million.

Δ   Permitting a spouse who has a separate trust with assets in excess of $600,000 to provide for his/her surviving spouse and to defer estate taxes.

Why consider a tax planning living trust?

Reducing federal estate taxes and avoiding probate are the primary reasons for using a tax planning living trust. A will containing tax planning provisions can save estate taxes, but the expense and delay of probate is also involved. A tax planning living trust will save the same amount of taxes and avoid probate, doubling the benefit for your family. To avoid any confusion, we need to review the two kinds of taxes that must be paid when you die - *income taxes and estate taxes*.

Income taxes

Your estate must file a final *federal* income tax return just as you do each year, regardless of whether or not you have a living trust. Most states will also require a final *state* income tax return to be filed. All income received by you in the year you die must be reported and any taxes owed on that income must be paid. Your living trust has no effect on your income taxes.

Estate taxes

The other tax is the "federal estate tax," also known as the "death tax." If the *net* value of your estate (the fair market value of all your assets less your debts) exceeds $600,000 when you die, then your estate must pay federal estate taxes before any distribution is made to your beneficiaries. The federal estate tax on the *first* $600,000 is $192,800, however everyone receives a tax *credit* of $192,800 which means the first $600,000 is exempt from estate taxes. We will refer to this as the $600,000 exemption.

FEDERAL ESTATE TAX*

ESTATE SIZE	ESTATE TAX	% OF ESTATE TAKEN
$0 - 600,000	$ 0	0%
700,000	37,000	5.3%
800,000	75,000	9.4%
900,000	114,000	12.6%
1,000,000	153,000	15.3%
1,100,000	194,000	17.6%
1,200,000	235,000	19.6%
* Currently you pay no federal estate taxes on the first $600,000 you own. Any amount over $600,000 is taxed at 37-55%.		

The federal estate tax rate starts at 37%. This can be very expensive as you can see on the above chart. The estate tax is due within nine months of your death and must be paid in cash. This means that real estate, farms, family businesses, antiques, heirlooms, and other assets often have to be sold quickly at "fire sale" prices to pay estate taxes.

Be aware that some states also collect a state death tax (also called an "inheritance tax"). A discussion of state inheritance taxes is beyond the scope of this book. Your tax preparer can help you estimate your state death tax liability.

The estate tax is actually a double tax. Through the years, you have already paid income taxes on the assets that comprise your estate. And your estate may have to pay taxes on these assets again unless you plan ahead. A properly planned living trust can reduce these estate taxes.

Determining your net estate

You should determine your net estate before you decide whether or not you need a tax planning living trust. The easy to use Information Form at the end of this book will help you calculate your net estate.

Your net estate is determined by adding up the current market value of everything you own, minus any debts, mortgage, and charitable contributions. Your estate includes the death benefits from all life or term insurance policies on your life (or others) over which you have any "incidents of ownership," as defined by the IRS. This includes policies for which you have the right to name and change the beneficiary, borrow against the policy, or assign it, regardless of *who* actually owns the policy and even if the death benefits are paid to someone other than your estate. Also included are policies for which your employer pays the premiums and you have the right to name and change the beneficiary.

For example, assume your net estate is $500,000. You also have a life insurance policy with a $200,000 death benefit payable to your son. Because you owned the policy when you died and since you had the right to change the beneficiary, the $200,000 death benefit is included in your estate despite the fact that the proceeds will be paid directly to your son. As a result, your taxable estate is calculated at $700,000 by the IRS, resulting in a $37,000 federal estate tax.

It is very important for you to understand that the full death benefit of anything you own or have the right to change the beneficiary of is included in your taxable estate. Many persons are much closer to $600,000 than they realize, especially after including insurance death proceeds.

Uncle Sam created the "marital deduction" plan exclusively for married persons. Here is how it works: You, as a married person, can leave an *unlimited amount* of property to your spouse (provided he/she is a U.S. citizen) at your death without having to pay any federal estate tax. Under Uncle's marital deduction plan, no federal estate taxes are due when the first spouse dies.

So far this sounds great. But when the surviving spouse dies, the full value of the estate (including *what you* left your spouse and your spouse's own property) will be taxed *before* it can be distributed to the beneficiaries. The surviving spouse's estate is entitled to an estate tax credit equal to a $600,000 net estate, so the first $600,000 of the estate can go to the heirs tax-free, *but any excess is taxed*. The following example may help you to better understand how the marital deduction works.

Assume a husband and wife have a $1.2 million estate. The husband dies leaving all of his property to his wife. Under the marital deduction plan, no estate tax is due. Then the wife dies. Her estate is valued at $1.2 million (her original share plus what her husband transferred to her by the marital deduction). Now look what happens!

No federal estate taxes are due when the first spouse dies

SURVIVING SPOUSE	
$ 600,000	Wife's original share
+ 600,000	Deceased husband's share transferred to wife by marital deduction (no estate taxes)
1,200,000	Estate value at wife's death
- 600,000	Wife's federal estate tax exemption
600,000	Wife's taxable estate
$ 235,000	**Federal estate tax owed**

The marital deduction plan works fine when the first spouse dies because there is no estate tax liability for property transfers between spouses at death. The problem arises when the surviving spouse dies. In this case, a $235,000 estate tax is owed at the death of the surviving spouse because her estate value exceeded her estate tax exemption by $600,000.

But guess what? Each spouse is entitled to a $600,000 net estate exempt from tax, if they plan ahead. They could have passed up to $1.2 million to their heirs tax-free, but now the estate is only entitled to one $600,000 exemption (the surviving spouse's exemption) because the husband didn't use his exemption. Uncle Sam is very patient (and smart)—he'll wait until the surviving spouse dies and collect more taxes on a much larger estate.

Once again, you have a choice. You can do nothing and use Uncle Sam's plan. Or you can use your living trust to reduce or eliminate taxes *and* avoid probate.

Remember too, that people today are living longer (women generally outlive their husbands by many years) and even a modest estate can appreciate greatly over time, especially if you own real estate or investments, or if you have large amounts of life insurance.

TAX PLANNING LIVING TRUSTS

Use your

living trust

to reduce

or

eliminate

taxes and

avoid

probate

Before we go any further, we should explain that a tax planning trust is a revocable living trust (as we discussed in *Part 2*), with additional special provisions required by the IRS so that each spouse's $600,000 estate tax exemption is preserved.

Tax planning living trusts are based on the fact that *each spouse* is entitled to a $600,000 exemption. A husband and wife can pass up to $1.2 million to their heirs tax-free, provided they plan ahead with their living trust while they are both still alive and competent.

Common trusts vs. separate trusts

Spouses wanting to reduce or eliminate federal estate taxes have the option of creating a separate trust for each spouse and having separate estates while they are both still alive or they can use a "common" trust.

Most married couples own their property together and usually prefer having one "common" tax planning trust. This option is much simpler and more practical than establishing separate trusts and dividing all of the marital property into "his" and "hers" while both spouses are alive. *All* of the marital property is held inside of one common tax planning trust. It is not divided until one spouse dies.

If you want to pursue the common trust approach, don't get confused or sidetracked by using the wrong name. Even though they may look the same, a common tax trust is very different from a "joint" living trust.

With a common living trust each spouse owns a *one-half* undivided interest in each trust asset. This happens automatically as property is put into the trust. When the first spouse dies, each trust asset is "split right down the middle" giving each spouse one-half of the estate. By comparison, *all* of the property in a joint living trust is owned by the surviving spouse when the first spouse dies. Make certain you explain to your attorney that you want a *common* tax planning trust.

You and your spouse also have the option of using separate trusts. Most attorneys will recommend this because they either aren't familiar with the common tax trust or they prefer to use separate trusts. The estate tax savings will be the same, but all of your marital property will have to be divided and put into each separate trust while both spouses are alive. This can be very complicated and not at all how most married people like to handle their business. For example, in whose trust do you put your home, stocks, bank accounts, cars, etc.? Separate tax trusts are most often found in remarriage situations, where the spouses have always held their assets separately, or where one spouse has separate property he/she wants to keep out of the marriage.

Only married persons can use a tax planning trust

THERE ARE THREE TYPES OF TAX PLANNING REVOCABLE LIVING TRUSTS

AB common trust: Recommended for estates between $600,000 and $1.2 million or for larger estates where the couple wishes to maximize the amount of control given to the surviving spouse. The AB trust is sometimes referred to as the "By-pass trust" or the "Credit Shelter trust." It is the most popular tax planning trust.

QTIP common trust: Recommended for estates exceeding $1.2 million. It is also called the "ABC" trust.

QTIP separate trust: Recommended for married persons with a separate estate in excess of $600,000. It is a separate trust. This trust is also known as the "BC" trust.

AB Common Tax Trust

A common AB trust gives each spouse a one-half undivided interest in the trust property. All of the property is titled in the name of the common trust, which usually names both spouses as co-trustees. Upon the death of the first spouse, the surviving spouse divides all of the trust property into two shares. This does not require writing two new trusts, but does require keeping two separate ledgers to account for the property which has been retitled into each trust share.

The surviving spouse can be the trustee of the marital trust and of the family trust

One share—known as the "A" or "marital trust"—belongs to the surviving spouse as his/her property. This share remains revocable, meaning the surviving spouse has control of the marital trust property. The marital trust is not taxed until the surviving spouse dies.

The other share—known as the "B" or "family trust"—is made up of the deceased spouse's one-half share, up to $600,000. Any excess amount is placed into the marital trust by use of the marital deduction between spouses. Unlike the marital trust, the family trust is "irrevocable," meaning its provisions and beneficiaries cannot be changed by the surviving spouse. This protects the family trust assets if the surviving spouse remarries or changes the provisions of the marital trust. Since the family trust does not exceed $600,000, the amount of the federal estate tax exemption, no federal estate tax is due at the death of the first spouse. No estate taxes will be assessed against the family trust even if it increases in value during the lifetime of the surviving spouse. Its assets will ultimately pass to the beneficiaries free of estate taxes.

The surviving spouse can be the trustee of the marital trust and of the family trust, ensuring total management and investment control for the survivor. A family member or a corporate trustee can also be named as trustee (or co-trustee) of the family trust. Typically, all of the family trust income is given to the surviving spouse during his/her lifetime, but the trust can be written so the surviving spouse receives no family trust income or a restricted income.

The surviving spouse can also be given the right to "invade" the family trust principal for his/her support, medical care and education if he/she runs short of funds in the marital trust and needs money for normal living expenses. There are some restrictions if the surviving spouse takes money from the family trust for other reasons, but these areas cover anything the survivor would generally need. The surviving spouse cannot have 100% control over the assets in the family trust, because that would legally give him/her ownership of them causing them to be taxed when the survivor dies.

So, for the rest of the surviving spouse's life, he/she has complete control over his/her own trust, plus he/she gets all the income from the family trust and can withdraw principal from it when needed. And when the surviving spouse dies, the assets in both trusts (up to $600,000 each, a total of $1.2 million) will pass to the beneficiaries tax-free and without probate. What could be better than that?

The right to invade can be restricted or even eliminated. A properly planned AB trust will not allow the surviving spouse, as trustee of the family trust, to make a discretionary payment of income or principal to himself/herself. Instead, the trust should require that the decision be made by the other co-trustee. If there is no co-trustee, then the trust should require that the decision be made by the next successor trustee who becomes a permanent co-trustee to act with the surviving spouse.

Special provisions can be included in the AB trust (and the other tax trusts explained below) so the principal of the family trust cannot be invaded for catastrophic illness costs of the surviving spouse. For example, only the marital trust would have to be "spent down" to qualify the surviving spouse for Medicaid benefits, preserving the assets in the family trust for the beneficiaries. You should know that these provisions may not work if they are not correctly worded or Congress changes the laws in this area. We'll discuss this more in a moment.

At the death of the surviving spouse, the property in the family trust must be distributed to the deceased spouse's beneficiaries. The marital trust property is distributed to the surviving spouse's beneficiaries who may be the same as for the family trust, or different if the surviving spouse made any changes.

An AB trust allows a husband and wife to pass $1.2 million to their heirs without any federal estate taxes—$600,000 at the death of the first spouse (even though the surviving spouse may have an interest in this share) and $600,000 at the death of the surviving spouse. The following chart shows how an AB trust works on an estate of $1.2 million.

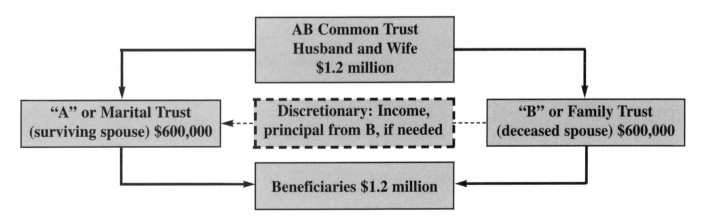

Result: No Probate. Beneficiaries receive $1.2 million and avoid all federal estate tax.

An AB trust offers the benefit of equal control for each spouse

Advantages: Besides avoiding probate, providing for the surviving spouse and allowing married persons to pass $1.2 million to their heirs without any federal estate tax, an AB trust offers the benefit of equal control for each spouse. One-half of the common estate is placed into the deceased spouse's family trust, which is irrevocable and cannot be changed by the surviving spouse. This allows the first spouse to die to maintain control over one-half of the common assets.

The AB trust gives each spouse equal control even if the common estate is *less* than $600,000. For example, using the AB trust for a $400,000 estate would leave $200,000 in the family trust and $200,000 in the marital trust at the death of the first spouse, who keeps control of one-half of the estate. Interestingly, the AB trust is increasingly used by married persons *without any federal estate tax liability* for the express purpose of giving each spouse *equal control of the estate*.

If the estate is larger than $1.2 million, then the AB trust will allow the survivor control of *more* than one-half of the estate. This may be acceptable if the spouses want the survivor to control as much of the property as possible, but if the spouses want to maintain equal control beyond $1.2 million, then they will need to use the QTIP tax planning trust discussed below.

QTIP Common Tax Trust

The QTIP common tax trust, also known as the ABC tax planning trust, is used for estates larger than $1.2 million. A QTIP trust does *not* save federal estate taxes beyond the $1.2 million permitted to a husband and wife. It lets each spouse control one-half of the portion of the estate which exceeds $1.2 million, and it defers federal estate taxes.

In the AB trust, once the estate exceeds $1.2 million, the surviving spouse will receive and then control more assets than the deceased spouse. For example, a $1.6 million estate using an AB trust will be divided at the death of the first spouse by placing $600,000 into the family trust and $1 million into the marital trust. Since the marital trust is still revocable, the surviving spouse controls more than one-half of the estate.

Congress created the QTIP trust to solve the problem of unequal control between spouses. QTIP means "qualified terminable interest property." This sounds very complicated, but it really isn't. This is how the QTIP trust works with a $1.6 million estate.

At the death of the first spouse, the estate is divided in half so $800,000 goes into the marital trust owned by the surviving spouse. The remaining one-half, or $800,000 belonging to the deceased spouse, is then divided into two shares. The first share is placed into the family trust and will not exceed $600,000, because this is the amount of the federal estate tax exemption. The *excess*, or $200,000, is placed into a third trust called the "C" or "QTIP" trust. The following chart will help you understand how a QTIP trust works with a $1.6 million estate.

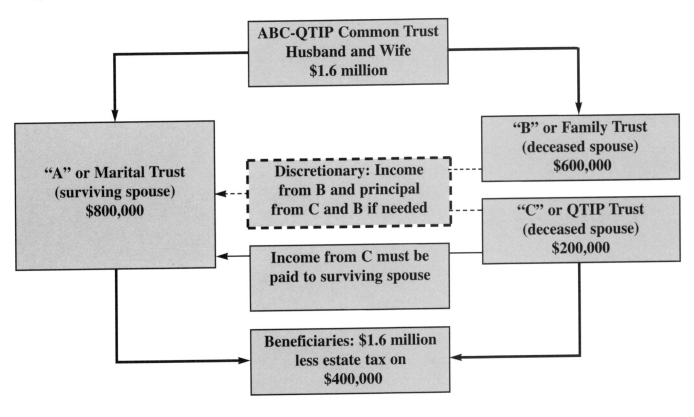

Result: No probate. Beneficiaries receive $1.2 million free of federal estate tax. Estate taxes on $400,000 (excess over $1.2 million) are deferred until death of surviving spouse.

Since the family trust does not exceed $600,000, the amount of the federal estate tax exemption, no tax is due at the death of the first spouse. Estate taxes on the QTIP trust share are deferred until the surviving spouse dies. The marital and QTIP trust shares are included in the surviving spouse's estate.

In our example, the taxable estate at the death of the surviving spouse is $1 million, made up of $800,000 in the marital trust and $200,000 in the QTIP trust share. After the surviving spouse's $600,000 exemption is applied, federal estate taxes of $153,000 are owed on the $400,000 excess. This amount is paid based on the amount of tax generated by each trust share ($75,000 by the marital share and $78,000 by the QTIP share), unless the trust specifies a different formula for allocating the estate tax liability between the two trust shares.

The surviving spouse has complete control over the marital trust. Under IRS regulations *all* of the income from the QTIP trust *must* be paid to the surviving spouse. The survivor can also be paid the income from the family trust and be given the right to invade the principal of both the QTIP and the family trust shares for his/her support, medical care and education. A QTIP tax planning trust, like the AB trust, may also be written so the family trust income and the right to invade the principal of the QTIP trust share or the family trust share is restricted or prohibited.

The surviving spouse divides the original trust assets between the three trust shares and can be the trustee of all three trusts. Like the AB trust, the QTIP can be set up so that the principal of the QTIP trust share and the principal of the family trust share can receive limited protection from the catastrophic illness costs of the surviving spouse.

Advantages: Besides avoiding probate, providing for the surviving spouse and allowing married persons to pass $1.2 million estate tax free to their beneficiaries, a QTIP trust offers these benefits:

Equal control for first to die: One-half of the common estate is placed into the deceased spouse's family and QTIP trust shares. These trusts are *irrevocable,* and cannot be changed by the surviving spouse, so the first spouse to die retains equal control.

Defer estate taxes: The QTIP trust share is not taxed until the surviving spouse dies. This keeps the estate intact so a greater amount is available to produce income and principal, if needed, for the surviving spouse during his/her lifetime.

QTIP Separate Tax Trust

This trust, also known as the "BC" or "BC-QTIP trust," is for a married person having a *separate* estate in excess of $600,000. It is commonly used in a remarriage situation where one spouse has substantially more property than the other spouse or when the spouses want to use separate trusts.

The QTIP separate trust eliminates probate, allows control of separate assets after death, provides for a surviving spouse, and defers estate taxes

The QTIP tax trust can defer estate taxes

until the death of the surviving spouse. The following chart will show how a QTIP separate trust trust works with a married person who owns $800,000 of separate property.

When the trust owner dies, the trust is divided into two shares the "B" or *family* trust share and the "C" or *QTIP* trust share. The family trust is funded with assets equal in value to the federal estate tax exemption or $600,000. The excess or $200,000 is put into the QTIP trust share.

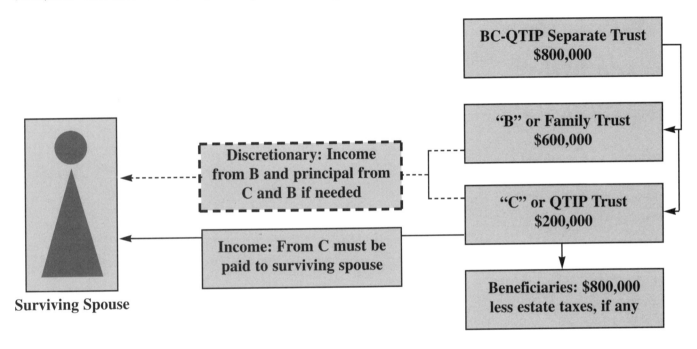

Surviving Spouse

Result: No probate. Beneficiaries receive $600,000 free of federal estate tax. Estate taxes on $200,000 (excess over $600,000) are deferred until death of surviving spouse.

The family trust has no estate tax liability because its value is $600,000, the amount of the estate tax exemption. Estate taxes are deferred on the QTIP trust share until the surviving spouse dies.

The family trust and the QTIP trust share are irrevocable. All of the net income from the QTIP trust share *must* be paid to the surviving spouse for his/her lifetime. In addition, the trust may be set up to allow the surviving spouse to receive the net income from the family trust and principal from both the QTIP and the family trust shares for his/her support, medical care and education. When the surviving spouse dies, the property in both trust shares is distributed to the beneficiaries of the first spouse.

The QTIP separate tax trust is commonly used in a remarriage

Your surviving spouse can be trustee of the family trust and the QTIP trust, but since this trust usually contains your separate property, you might not want your spouse to be the trustee of it—and would instead name a family member or a corporate trustee.

The QTIP separate trust offers another important benefit: it allows the deferred estate tax liability on the QTIP trust to be eliminated if the *survivor* has a small estate. Using our example, let's assume the surviving spouse has a $200,000 separate estate when he/she dies. The taxable estate is $400,000—$200,000 in separate property *plus* the $200,000 in the deceased spouse's QTIP trust. Since the surviving spouse's exemption amount is $600,000, the $400,000 is free of estate tax. The first spouse's $600,000 *exemption* protects the family trust share. In effect, the $200,000 QTIP share "borrows" a portion of the *unused* surviving spouse's $600,000 exemption. So the entire $800,000 estate is protected from the estate tax. This means that both spouses transfer a total of $1 million to their respective beneficiaries tax free.

The QTIP separate trust can be set up so that the principal of the family trust and the principal of the QTIP trust receive limited protection from invasion for the catastrophic illness costs of the surviving spouse. This preserves the deceased spouse's separate estate for his/her beneficiaries.

Advantages: Like the AB trust and the ABC trust, a BC-QTIP trust avoids probate and can provide for the needs of the surviving spouse. It also offers the following benefits:

Complete control of separate assets: At the death of the spouse/owner, the family trust and the QTIP trust shares become irrevocable. This means that the spouse/owner has complete control over his/her separate property after death.

Defer estate taxes: The QTIP trust share is not taxed until the surviving spouse dies, keeping the estate intact so more assets are available to produce income and principal, if needed, for the surviving spouse during his/her lifetime.

If Your Spouse Is Not A U.S. Citizen

A non-citizen spouse is no longer entitled to the unlimited marital deduction. This means that without additional planning, the *citizen* spouse's estate will be taxed if it exceeds $600,000 before distribution to the *non-citizen* spouse. This problem can be solved by using a QTIP common or a QTIP separate trust containing special provisions which allow the trust to qualify under IRS regulations as a "qualified domestic trust" also called a "QDOT." You should also know that, effective July 14, 1988, a citizen spouse cannot transfer more than $100,000 *per year* to the non-citizen spouse (including consideration in the form of debt reduction), without incurring a tax liability. To avoid problems, consult with a professional specializing in this area *before* you transfer any property to your non-citizen spouse or set up a tax planning living trust.

What About Using A Will With Tax Planning Provisions?

You may have heard of estate tax planners who incorporate "tax planning trusts" into a will to reduce estate taxes in much the same way as a tax planning living trust. But watch out—*a will must be probated before the trusts can go into effect*—so you haven't avoided probate. By the time the trust goes into effect, a portion of your estate is lost to probate costs, not to mention all the other problems that accompany probate. **With a living trust you can reduce estate taxes without probate.**

CATASTROPHIC ILLNESS AND MEDICAID "SPEND DOWN"

A tax planning living trust does not guarantee protection against Medicaid spend down requirements for catastrophic illness. Congress is always changing the laws in this area and the trend is to increasingly restrict the use of trusts to avoid the medicaid spend down provisions. It is very probable that Congress will eventually disallow them. Medicaid spend down protections, like the special needs trust we previously discussed, should always be considered limited protection.

Use these special provisions if they benefit your situation, but be aware that they may not work the way you hope. The medicaid laws are very complex and constantly changing so make certain your attorney is experienced in this area and periodically reviews your trust.

SETTLING A TAX PLANNING LIVING TRUST

Your trustee has a legal duty to follow detailed IRS procedures at the death of *each* spouse in order to take advantage of the estate tax savings. These requirements are in addition to the basic trust settlement procedures such as paying bills, distributing assets, etc. For example, your trustee must correctly divide the trust property into the trust shares (marital trust, family trust, QTIP trust) required by the type of tax trust you used, apply for a new tax identification number for the family trust (and QTIP trust), and prepare and file the appropriate federal and state estate tax returns. The estate tax savings may be lost and substantial costs and penalties may result if the IRS procedures are not followed, so it is very important that your tax trust be settled correctly.

Your trustee has a legal responsibility to hire a competent professional (an experienced accountant, CPA, or tax attorney) if the trustee feels he/she lacks the experience to settle the trust. A properly prepared trust will authorize the trustee to hire outside professionals if the trustee thinks they are needed. Remember, your trustee can be held *personally* liable to the beneficiaries of your trust for lost tax savings, audit and legal fees, and penalties, if the settlement isn't done correctly.

Costs of settling a tax planning trust will vary depending on your situation, where you live and the professional used. We recommend that you budget approximately $1,000 - $2,000 at the death of *each* spouse. These estimates do not include appraisal costs or tax audit expenses. Tax planning trusts require additional paperwork and documentation in order to capture the federal estate tax savings produced by your trust. These costs (which are deductible expenses) are nominal compared to the potential estate tax savings. For example, under current law a properly prepared tax trust will generate a $37,000 savings on a $700,000 estate, so it pays to settle your trust correctly.

Settling a tax planning trust is *primarily* an accounting function, so we recommend using an experienced CPA or tax attorney to settle your tax trust. (Just make sure he/she has experience in this area.) In many cases this person is already handling your income tax returns and is familiar with your situation so they will be more efficient (and less expensive) than someone who doesn't know you. Many accountants and CPA's routinely handle all of the accounting and tax paperwork, then hire an attorney to review what they have done and write an opinion letter verifying that everything has been prepared according to the trust instructions and IRS regulations. We recommend that you contact a professional after you set up your tax planning trust to review your situation and give you a cost estimate for settling your tax trust. This can save your trustee time and money later on.

No one can guarantee that your trust will not be audited. Obviously, thorough and accurate settlement documentation reduces the likelihood of an audit and improves the chances that your trust will be able to successfully pass an audit. Audits may result in additional fees. Your trust will be responsible for audit costs, including penalties and interest.

Settling a tax planning trust is primarily an accounting function

Listed below are some of the special procedures required by a tax planning living trust at the death of the first spouse. The same procedures are followed at the death of the second spouse, except for the division of property into the appropriate trust shares.

These requirements are *not* the result of choosing to do a tax planning living trust. As we earlier explained, estate tax planning can be done through a will or a living trust. In either case the IRS settlement procedures are the same. But by using the living trust, you have eliminated the cost and delay of probate in addition to reducing or eliminating your estate taxes.

Checklist For Settling A Tax Planning Living Trust

Δ   Inventory all assets (including detailed listing of all safe deposit box contents) and determine all liabilities (personal loans, debts, mortgages, etc.).

Δ   Establish fair market value of all assets, including personal property. Secure independent appraisals, if necessary.

Δ   Apply for federal tax identification number for the family trust (and the QTIP trust, if applicable).

Δ   Divide the property into the family trust and the marital trust (and the QTIP trust, if applicable).

Δ   File appropriate federal estate tax return and, if required, state estate tax return.

Δ   File appropriate federal and state decedent final income tax returns.

Δ   Retitle assets into the separate name of the Family Trust and Marital Trust (and the QTIP Trust, if applicable).

Your revocable living trust should always be the foundation of your estate plan

BEYOND YOUR TAX PLANNING LIVING TRUST

If you are married with a common estate larger than $1.2 million or are a single person with an estate larger than $600,000, you may wish to consider additional estate tax planning options to further reduce or eliminate your estate tax liability. These options are in *addition* to your basic living trust plan. They do not replace it. Your *revocable* living trust should always be the foundation of your estate plan.

All of these additional options are "irrevocable" (they cannot be changed or revoked) once they have been set up. They all require you to legally give up ownership of your property, so think very carefully *before* you sign any irrevocable legal documents. Once you give your property away, it's gone forever. Remember: you cannot change your mind later on and take your property back even in the event that you need it, your financial situation has deteriorated, or catastrophic illness has occurred, etc.

Irrevocable options can be used to produce income for you and your family during your lifetime and to pass assets, free from estate taxes, to family or favorite charities while satisfying IRS requirements.

HERE ARE THE MOST COMMON IRREVOCABLE TAX PLANNING OPTIONS

Gifting

Irrevocable Life Insurance Trust

Family Limited Partnership

Charitable Remainder Trust

Charitable Lead Trust

Charitable Contributions

Grantor Retained Income Trust (GRIT)

A discussion of these irrevocable options is outside the scope of this book. You should know that estate tax planning beyond the basic tax planning living trust involves complex and constantly changing areas of the law. The IRS rules and reporting requirements are very technical and very strict. In addition, the IRS will very likely audit anyone using irrevocable options. Your plan must be properly set up or you can lose the tax savings *and* be assessed penalties and interest if the IRS audits and disallows your plan. This is definitely *not* a job for amateurs or general practitioners. Seek expert advice by consulting with an attorney or a CPA who specializes in estate tax planning and is thoroughly knowledgeable of the irrevocable options *before* you make any gifts or transfer your property into any irrevocable legal document. A specialist can evaluate your particular situation, explain your options, recommend the irrevocable plans most beneficial for your tax situation and make certain your plan satisfies IRS requirements.

Some Final Words On Estate Planning

Many people never do any estate planning because they get lost in the complexities of trying to understand every possible planning option. This is a difficult and frustrating approach which makes it very easy to procrastinate.

Plan your estate in a logical order—from basic to complex. Start with setting up a basic living trust (or tax planning trust) to completely avoid probate and reduce or eliminate federal estate taxes. Since a foundation living trust estate plan will handle most people's needs, you don't need to waste additional time collecting information about options that are not relevant to your situation.

It's very important that you *take action now* and set up your basic plan first so that you and your family will be protected. You can always "fine tune" your plan with one or more irrevocable options later on without affecting your foundation living trust estate plan.

Plan your estate in a logical order— from basic to complex

When any good product falls into "bad hands," abuses and scams can occur. Unfortunately, the increasing popularity of living trusts has attracted the attention of some who see this as a quick way to make a fast buck. We feel a responsibility to educate you about the most common living trust abuses and scams so you can protect yourself, your family and your property.

Please don't deny yourself the benefits provided by a properly prepared living trust estate plan just because a few opportunistic people misuse a good product. We've included this section in our expanded second edition so that you will be an informed and confident consumer. You may also wish to review the section on finding the right attorney.

One blatant misrepresentation that occurs is the sale of inferior quality living trusts through trust marketing companies. Traveling sales representatives are knocking on doors across the country and using high pressure sales tactics to sell mass-produced poor quality form trusts at grossly inflated prices. Most of these salespersons know nothing about living trusts—they are hired and paid based on their ability to close a sale. And they are paid a commission based on the number of trusts they sell—they're after quantity, not quality. They have to sell a great many trusts because the revenue generated from each sale is split between many people, especially in the trust marketing companies that are structured as "pyramids" or multi-level marketing operations. Attorney involvement is minimal, and sometimes an attorney is not even consulted. Many of these are no more than fly-by-night "boiler room" operations that openly violate consumer protection laws. Frequent violations involve practicing law without a license. Once they get your money, they often disappear, leaving you with a poor quality or defective trust. Sometimes they just "go south" with your money and you receive nothing.

Living trust abuses and scams such as these have become so widespread that the National Association of Attorneys General has organized a task force to combat deceptive sales of living trusts. More than 25 states have joined this task force.

Cross Selling

Another questionable practice regarding the sales of living trusts is known as "cross selling." Financial planners, stockbrokers, and insurance agents have jumped on the living trust "bandwagon" by capitalizing on the public's interest in living trust estate planning as a way to sell insurance, investments and the like. These activities are legal but ethically very "iffy." Here's how the cross-sellers operate:

Attorneys, insurance agents, stockbrokers, financial planners, cemetery salespersons, bankers and other marketing firms often co-sponsor living trust seminars. They advertise in the newspaper or by direct mail that you can attend a seminar on using a living trust to avoid probate and eliminate estate taxes. In reality, this is the "bait" to catch your attention and get you in the front door since most people already have their own insurance agents or financial advisors and are not interested in attending seminars on those subjects.

The speaker is usually an attorney, but not always. Seminar sponsors frequently hire a non-lawyer out-of-town living trust "expert" or "specialist" to make a living trust presentation. These experts and specialists are not attorneys and are not qualified to give legal advice. Their objective is to sell you a trust as quickly as possible by presenting a slick sales pitch. Other speakers will discuss insurance, investments, financial planning, pre-need burial plans and so forth. You will be told that a "team" approach is required to properly set up a living trust. The team will evaluate your investments and insurance. They will also assist you in retitling your property to the trust name. Of course, the recommended team members just happen to be the same persons who co-sponsored the seminar. You may be quoted a package price if you hire the team. This price is often "reduced" if you sign up at the seminar. The fee is inflated, because it has to be split between the team members to help pay for the cost of the seminar.

Expect any question and answer period to be short and the answers vague, especially to the question of "how much is this going to cost me?" To get your questions answered, you will be encouraged to schedule a private meeting with one or more of the team members. They will ask you to complete a detailed financial questionnaire—to share with all of the team members—as the first step to setting up your trust. This lets them review all of your personal information which they will use to recommend that you purchase additional investments, insurance, and services when you set up your trust.

Cross selling is easily abused and can significantly increase your trust preparation expenses. For example, a team member may want to charge you a fee to "analyze" your financial situation *before* you see the attorney. This is absolutely unnecessary because your attorney will confidentially review your situation when he/she helps you set up your

You don't need a "team" to help you set up your trust

trust. This cost is included in the legal fee, so don't pay for something you don't need.

Be suspicious of living trust seminars sponsored by companies selling insurance and other investments. After all, why would an insurance agent promote a living trust seminar unless it created an opportunity to sell insurance? Be cautious and use your time efficiently. Attend a living trust seminar to learn about living trusts. Don't waste time with things you aren't interested in or don't need. And don't be conned into believing that setting up your living trust requires you to purchase additional investments and insurance or that you must do business with any company other than the ones you presently use. You don't need a "team" to help you set up your trust; the *right* attorney is all you need. Afterwards *your* attorney, insurance agent, stockbroker, banker, etc., can easily assist you in retitling your property to the trust name. All companies follow the same retitling procedures, so you don't have to get involved with anyone new. Stick with the people you do business with right now.

Trust Sales Companies

Trust "sales" companies should not be confused with *regulated* trust companies which are legally authorized to manage trust assets and are strictly regulated by federal and state laws. Regulated trust companies are usually associated with a bank or stock brokerage company. They do not sell or prepare living trust documents; they consider this a conflict of interest. Legitimate trust companies charge a trustee fee for *managing* trust assets not for *selling* living trusts.

Companies selling living trusts through seminars, direct mail and door-to-door solicitations are not regulated, and their sales agents are not required to be attorneys or licensed or certified. As you can imagine, this lack of regulation has caused many problems: misleading/deceptive advertising, practicing law without a license, violating consumer protection laws, charging exorbitant fees for poor quality trusts, collecting fees without even preparing the trust documents, and making false claims about the benefits of a living trust (such as not having to pay income taxes), just to name a few of the most common complaints. These companies target the elderly and intimidate them with high pressure sales tactics.

An unregulated trust company is not a law firm, and its non-lawyer sales force is not qualified to give you legal advice about setting up a living trust estate plan or to answer your legal questions. To appear credible, these companies commonly disguise themselves so you will assume they are a law firm or a regulated trust company. They frequently have names which are very similar to the names of well-known and reputable organizations (or they infer that they are endorsed by these organizations). These tactics are intended to fool you so the sales agent can gain your confidence and make a quick sale.

Here is how the process usually works: The sales agent often has no established office and offers to meet with you in your home where he/she makes a sales presentation. The living trust price may be discounted, provided you sign up right then. If you do sign up, then the agent collects the fee and completes a questionnaire. The questionnaire is sent to the place where the documents are prepared—most often to an out-of-state location. Some companies contract with an attorney to "mass produce" trust documents. The company pays the attorney a set fee for each trust—two to three hundred dollars is common. (The balance of the inflated fee goes to sales commissions and the trust company.) It is unethical, an obvious conflict of interest, when the attorney is paid by the trust company to prepare your living trust. Who is the attorney's client—you or the trust company? The attorney prepares the trust documents from the information you provided to the sales agent, but the preparation process amounts to little more than inserting the information you provided to the sales agent into generic fill-in-the-blank trust forms. These operations are called "trust mills" because they have a reputation for churning out poor quality "cookie-cutter" trust documents. This is not what you want for your family.

There is rarely any direct contact between you and the attorney (who is accessible only through the sales agent). So it's easy to make mistakes or overlook something important. Since the attorney's fee is so low, he/she has no incentive to be personally involved in the preparation of your trust. Many trust mill attorneys delegate the trust preparation to paralegals or legal assistants so all they have to do is give "rubber stamp" approval to the completed documents.

Some companies will send you a draft copy of the trust documents for your review and approval while others just send final documents. Documents may be delivered by the agent or mailed. Trust documents are written in "legalese" and, because you have no direct access to the attorney, you have no opportunity to ask questions and be certain that you understand what your trust says—or doesn't say. And signing something you don't understand can have disastrous consequences for you and your family.

There are other problems. The agent may provide you with minimal assistance in getting the trust documents signed and the property retitled. But most of the time all you get are generic instructions so the actual signing and retitling process is left entirely up to you. Since the agent is not an attorney or licensed, he/she is not qualified to answer your questions or assist you with the retitling. This can cause problems, especially if you don't understand the instructions or you have special circumstances. This means trust documents can be improperly signed (which can make the trust invalid) and assets may not be correctly titled (so they risk being probated). You may have unknowingly created serious problems for you and your family.

After you receive your documents the sales agent moves on to other trust prospects. And since he/she has already been paid their commission on your trust, they have no incentive to spend any more time with you. The trust company is not concerned with your questions because it already has your money. And because trust companies frequently go out of business, you can't depend on them to be there if you need help. Many people, after spending good money, end up with living trust documents they don't understand and questions they can't get answered. This is not what you want, and this is why we strongly recommend that you avoid trust companies.

Captive Trust Sales Companies

The "captive" trust sales company operates very much like the one we just discussed, but there are differences you need to know about. Unethical insurance agents, financial planners and stockbrokers use the captive trust company for the purpose of generating additional fees and selling more insurance, investments, etc. Here is how a captive trust company works:

The agent/broker sets up a company to prepare living trust documents. The company is owned by the agent/broker. "Captive" means that the company is controlled by the agent/broker. It is not a *regulated* trust company or a law firm. The agent/broker then solicits his/her clients to set up living trusts to be prepared by the captive trust company. Captive trust companies operate as trust mills mass-producing poor quality form documents from the information you have provided. You receive a "one size fits all" generic living trust which may not be suitable for your situation. It may be defective. The agent/broker receives a referral fee for each trust prepared by the trust company. Referral fees are also paid to other agents/brokers when their clients buy a trust from the captive company. Of course, you are not told about this.

Some agents/brokers offer the living trust to their clients at a very low cost, sometimes as little as a few hundred dollars. The low cost may be for the living trust alone, with additional fees for the pour-over will, power of attorney, health care directive, deed, etc. Others charge a greatly inflated fee. The agent/broker may even offer a free living trust—provided you buy a "package" of financial services, often costing several thousand dollars. It is unethical for an agent/broker to sell living trusts to their clients unless it is fully disclosed to the client. It's a conflict of interest for your agent/broker to receive a fee from the trust company at the same time he/she is being compensated for handling your regular business. Don't put your family at risk by having a captive trust company prepare your living trust. Find the right attorney, who will do the job right and work in *your* best interest.

Brokerage Company Trust Companies

Understand that stock brokerage companies are now authorized to offer regulated trust department services. They pay their stock brokers extra to pressure clients to set up living trusts which name the brokerage company as corporate trustee. Clients are encouraged to move all of their cash and investments to the brokerage company. This is a great way for them to build up the assets managed by their trust department—which means more trustee fees and commissions for the brokerage company. This tactic is also unethical and a conflict of interest for the stockbroker (and the brokerage company), unless a full disclosure is made to you.

Naming the brokerage company as trustee of your living trust can cause problems for you and your family. Remember that a corporate trustee will charge you a trustee fee as soon as they begin to act. This can be very costly—often amounting to hundreds of dollars per year—because the trustee fee is based on the value of the assets. So the more you have the greater the cost. This is an unnecessary expense. If you name *yourself* as trustee (as most people do) then you can completely avoid this expense. There are other problems. For example, assets that the brokerage company is not interested in, such as your home, cars, and personal effects are often left out of the trust, so they must be probated when you die or if you become incapacitated. The reason you set up a living trust is to avoid the very predicament they would put you in. Protect yourself and your family by making certain that you are fully informed *before* you name a brokerage company as trustee of your living trust.

Report suspected abuses and scams

Do not allow trust sales representatives in your home

Report Suspected Abuses and Scams

The best way to prevent living trust abuses and scams is to immediately report any suspicious activity or companies to your state Attorney General, the Better Business Bureau, and your local or state Bar Association. Your effort helps alert them to a possible problem so they can investigate and, if necessary, take action to stop the activity *before* consumers can be harmed. This will involve a little time and effort on your part, but it helps protect your community from deceptive sales practices.

Remember, once an unscrupulous sales agent has your money, it is almost impossible to get it back. Report questionable living trust sales activities so these operations can be shut down before they harm the public and possibly one of your family members.

Additional Precautions

Δ   Do not allow trust sales representatives in your home. You could be opening your door to con artists or even criminal activity. And avoid telephone solicitations. Protect your privacy and be suspicious of any company that does not have an established business office.

Δ   Resist high pressure sales tactics. Tell the sales agent that you want to think it over first. This gives you time to see if any complaints have been filed against the company. If the offer is a good value today, then it will be an equally good value tomorrow. This gives you time to be objective, get a second opinion and then make the right decision. Remember, we are talking about your family and property, so don't let yourself be pressured into a decision you'll regret.

Δ   Ask questions and take notes about the agent's qualifications and experience, how long he or she has been with the trust company, names of referrals, and who actually prepares the trust documents (lawyer, paralegal, or legal assistant). Be sure to ask about the cost and how much of the fee goes to the agent (and the trust company). Find out who services the trust once it is set up should you later have questions or need an amendment. Are there any additional costs for this?

Δ   If an agent solicits you with a sales pitch and you are tempted to buy, insist on a letter that puts all of the claims in writing. Most sales pitches are oral so it is easy for the agent to deny misrepresentations. Don't sign any form that contains blanks or has unchecked boxes.

Δ   Tell the sales agent in advance that you are going to tape record the meeting so you can better remember what was said. If the agent refuses, then you can assume the sales presentation violates consumer protection laws or involves practicing law without a license. Having a tape recording of the meeting will be very useful if you later decide the agent's program is questionable and should be reported.

Δ   Do not give the sales agent any of your personal financial information. This should always be confidential between you and your attorney. You could be creating some real risks for yourself later on if you don't know who your information is being given to or what it will be used for.

Δ   Avoid seminars that charge you a fee for admittance. Don't pay for the privilege of receiving basic living trust information and getting your questions answered.

It pays to find the right attorney

The Good Guys

We do not want you to think that all insurance agents, stockbrokers, financial planners, etc., make misrepresentations and use deceptive sales practices. It's not fair to condemn the entire profession because of the abusive acts of a few. Most of these people are competent and dedicated professionals. They know about living trusts and believe in them. They feel they have a moral and ethical responsibility to inform their clients about living trusts. They will recommend that their clients use an experienced living trust attorney to set up their trust.

In summary, remember, a living trust is a legal document and if it is not properly prepared, you and your family could end up in a disastrous situation. Your trust should be set up by an attorney, and you need to find the right attorney. Paying some sales representative with a persuasive pitch to prepare your living trust just because you don't like (or are afraid of) attorneys is like shooting yourself in the foot. Remember, this is your family and your property we're talking about—don't risk their well-being. It pays to shop around and find the right attorney to set up your living trust estate plan.

We hope we've told you enough about probate that you'll want to make sure you and your family are protected from it. And you should understand living trusts enough by now that you'll feel comfortable getting one for yourself. You may even find yourself telling your neighbors, friends and relatives all about the advantages of setting up a living trust estate plan—and we think that would be wonderful!

We have spent a great deal of time trying to make this book simple enough for everyone to understand, yet complete enough so that you can ask the questions that you should ask and, most importantly, so that you can make *informed* decisions.

Please share this book with the rest of your family, your friends and your co-workers. Better yet, send them a copy of their own! It could be one of the most valuable gifts you ever give to those you care about.

Don't postpone protecting your family. None of us can know when tragedy will strike, and once it does it's too late. A sudden tragic accident or illness can put you and/or your family under the control of the probate court for years. Now you know what that can mean—and you know how to prevent it with a living trust estate plan.

Please act now.

When Do I need to Update My Living Trust?

Update your living trust any time it no longer says what you want done. Any major change in your family such as marriage, divorce (especially if *you* divorce or remarry), death, adoption, birth, etc., should cause you to think about changing your trust. Your attorney is responsible for notifying you of any changes in the law or tax code that could affect your trust.

You should also consider changing your trust if one of your trustees or guardians can no longer fulfill his/her responsibilities, or if your financial situation changes substantially. Do not write on your original trust document. It must not be altered. Have your attorney prepare an amendment to your trust that will be signed by you and notarized.

Where Should I Keep My Living Trust Document?

Expect to receive two original living trust documents. Keep one in your safe deposit box or a similar secure place. Make sure that your safe deposit box is rented in your living trust name so your back-up trustee has access if something happens to you. Keep the other original with this book, at home, so you can review it from time to time. Never keep all of your original documents in the same place, because they could be misplaced, stolen, destroyed in a fire, etc.

Am I Required To Give A Copy Of My Trust To Anyone?

No, you do not need to give a copy of your trust to anyone nor do you need to file or record it anywhere to make it effective. However, you may want to discuss it thoroughly with each of your back-up trustees so they can be familiar with your plans. Consider removing the distribution provisions from any trust copy you give to your back-ups or family members. You may not want them to know how you have distributed your estate, *especially if you later change your mind.*

Some companies may want to see a copy of your trust when you add your trust name on your accounts. They will usually accept either a copy of your certificate of trust or copies of the first page and signature page of the trust to satisfy their requirements. If they insist upon having a copy of your entire trust, protect your privacy and don't allow them to copy your distribution provisions, or consider moving your business elsewhere.

Never keep all of your original documents in the same place

Living trusts are recognized in all 50 states

What If I Move To Another State?

Although living trusts are recognized in all 50 states, specific state laws (such as community property) can sometimes affect your trust. Take your documents to a living trust attorney (use the process on *Page 94* to find a new attorney) and have him/her "spot check" them to ensure that they conform to the laws of that state.

For the most part, states follow the same general rules. If something does need to be changed, you don't need to pay another attorney to "reinvent the wheel" by setting up a new trust. Make sure the only parts that are changed are those that need to be changed under the laws of that state.

What If I Buy Assets In Another State?

Before buying assets (especially real estate) in another state, make sure they can be titled in the same way as in your home state. Your attorney can tell you if the title you want to use is acceptable in that state.

Do I Have To Retitle My Property After I Set Up My Living Trust?

Yes. All of your property and beneficiary designations must be retitled in your trust name.

Who Should I List As Beneficiary On My Life Insurance?

Name your trust as the beneficiary. This directs that the death proceeds will be paid to your trust first and then distributed according to your instructions. If you own your life insurance, then also have your agent retitle the policy with your trust as the owner.

Is It Expensive To Transfer My Assets Into My Living Trust?

No. There should be very little cost—just the nominal expense of recording a real estate deed, issuing a new car title, and perhaps mailing expenses to have stock or bond certificates reissued.

What Do I Do With My Income Tax Deferred Savings?

Your trust *cannot* be the owner of your IRA, Keogh, 401(K), or qualified annuity, because it would destroy the tax deferred status. However, your trust *can* be named as beneficiary. If you are a single person, name your trust as *primary* beneficiary. If you are married, name your spouse as *primary* beneficiary and your trust as *contingent* beneficiary. This gives the surviving spouse the option of "rolling over" the proceeds into his/her IRA and deferring payment of income taxes. If your spouse does not survive you, the proceeds are paid to your trust.

What About Adding Other Persons On My Accounts, Deeds, Etc., After I Have Set Up My Living Trust?

Don't do it. Your living trust eliminates the need to have anyone else on your asset titles. Adding the trust name protects that asset from probate, while adding other names may destroy your trust protection and can expose you to a lawsuit or bankruptcy.

Can I Set Up A Living Trust Without A Bank?

Yes.

Do I Have To Change My Living Trust If My Daughter Remarries Or Divorces and Changes Her Name?

No. A properly prepared trust will identify all of your children as your children. They are still your children regardless of what name they use in the future, so no changes are necessary.

What About Instructions For My Funeral and Burial, Organ Donations, Etc.?

You don't need to put this type of information in your living trust. Since this information will be needed immediately if something happens to you, we suggest that you write your instructions in a separate dated letter and give copies to all of your family members and back-up trustees. This ensures that they will all know your wishes. You can then make changes to these instructions at any time without having to change your living trust document.

Is There Anything Bad About A Living Trust?

No. There are no *legal* disadvantages to a properly prepared living trust. It is a very traditional, well-proven estate planning tool that has been used successfully for centuries.

There are no legal disadvantages to a properly prepared living trust

Is A Living Trust Expensive?

Not compared to the costs of probate. Most people should be able to get a basic living trust for $600 to $800. Costs may vary depending on where you live, if you need special provisions, additional tax planning, etc.

I Don't Have Many Assets. Do I Need A Living Trust?

Yes. The *less* you have the *more* you should be concerned about unnecessary probate expenses. A smaller estate, for example, usually loses a greater percentage of its value to probate costs than a larger estate.

Should I Have An Attorney Set Up My Living Trust?

Definitely. Don't try to do it yourself—you could be creating some real problems later. If you try to copy someone else's trust document, then you may leave out something important in your situation or include something inappropriate for your situation. Remember, a living trust is a legal document, and this is *your family*. It's not worth the risk. You need to find the *right* attorney (preferably a *living trust attorney* who practices exclusively in living trust estate planning) to help you.

Are All Living Trust Documents The Same?

No. There is no "standard form" for a living trust. The quality of trust documents varies from attorney to attorney. Some attorneys use "generic" trust forms, which usually are not very detailed or organized. Living trust attorneys, on the other hand, often have developed their own comprehensive trust documents as a result of their extensive trust experience.

Should My Attorney Be Named In My Living Trust?

No. Your trust instructions can be carried out privately by your selected family members if you become incapacitated or die. It's also a conflict of interest for the attorney preparing your trust estate plan to create a future job for himself/herself.

Do I Have To Stay With The Attorney Who Prepared My Trust?

No. You are under no obligation to continue using the attorney who prepared your trust. Another attorney can work on your living trust—just make sure you select one experienced in living trusts.

Do I Lose Control Of The Assets I Put Into My Living Trust?

Absolutely not. Your living trust is *revocable.* You keep full control of your assets. As "trustee" and owner of your living trust, you can do everything you could before—buy and sell assets, make changes, even cancel your trust at any time. *Nothing changes but the names on the asset titles and beneficiary designations.*

If Something Happens To Me, Who Has Control?

In the case of married persons (who are usually co-trustees), either spouse can act if the other becomes incapacitated or dies. If something happens to both of you, or if you are single, then your back-up trustee will take over for you.

Are Living Trusts New?

No. The "modern" living trust was developed by the Franciscan Monks in A.D. 1224.

Will My Living Trust Protect My Estate From Nursing Home Costs If I Or My Spouse Suffer A Catastrophic Illness?

No. Some limited protection may be provided by using a tax planning trust, but only after one spouse has died.

Do I Lose My One-Time $125,000 Capital Gains Exemption If I Put My Home In My Living Trust?

No. You still qualify for the exemption when you sell your home.

Do I Have To Specifically List All Of My Assets In My Living Trust?

No. Adding your trust name on your asset titles and beneficiary designations automatically includes them in your trust. It is *not* necessary to list your assets in the trust document itself.

It is not necessary to list your assets in the trust document itself

What About Assets I Acquire After I Set Up My Trust?

Have the new asset titled in the trust name. You don't have to change anything in your trust documents.

What About Personal Property That Doesn't Have A Formal Title?

A properly prepared living trust will automatically assign all of your personal property—furniture, clothes, jewelry, and other personal effects—to the trust.

Are My Bank And Savings Accounts Still Insured If I Retitle Them In My Trust Name?

Yes. Any account you have that is insured by the FDIC will *continue* to be insured after you retitle it in your trust name—up to $100,000 per institution. Remember, all accounts titled in the trust name are combined for FDIC insurance coverage, so do not keep more than $100,000 at any one FDIC insured institution.

Does A Living Trust Affect My Income Taxes?

No. A living trust has no affect on the amount of income taxes you must pay.

Can A Living Trust Be Used To Reduce Or Eliminate Estate Taxes?

Yes. Only married couples can use a tax planning living trust.

Who Decides If I Am Mentally or Physically Incapacitated Enough For My Back-Up Trustee To Take Over?

You do. Your trust instructions will specify how many and what kinds of physicians must examine you and verify your ability to handle your business affairs. Your trust will also permit you to preselect your choice of physicians on a separate list signed by you, notarized and attached to your trust. This prevents "physician shopping" by unscrupulous relatives.

If I Set Up A Living Trust, What Happens To My Old Will?

When you sign your living trust documents (specifically your pour-over will), all previous wills are revoked.

Will A Living Trust Protect My Assets From Creditors?

No. Your trust assets are still subject to your debts and obligations.

Do I Have To Have A Separate Tax I.D. Number And File A Separate Income Tax Return For My Living Trust?

No. A revocable living trust does *not* require a separate tax I.D. number or the filing of a separate income tax return so long as at least one of the trust grantors is also acting as trustee. You will continue using your social security number and filing your individual income tax returns.

Do Married Persons Each Have To Have A Separate Living Trust?

No. Most married persons prefer to use a *joint* trust or a *common* tax planning trust. Separate trusts between spouses are most frequently found in a remarriage situation or when a spouse wants to keep certain assets as his/her separate property.

Do I Need The Permission Of My Mortgage Company To Transfer My Real Estate To My Living Trust?

No.

Will My Real Estate Be Reassessed If I Transfer It To My Living Trust?

No.

Will I Have To Pay Taxes on the Assets I Transfer To My Living Trust?

No new taxes result from creating and funding your trust.

What Happens If One Of Our Living Trust Beneficiaries Should Die Before We Do?

Your trust should provide for that contingency by indicating how the deceased beneficiary's share is to be distributed.

No new taxes result from creating and funding your trust

I'm A Single Person. Can I Use A Tax Planning Living Trust To Reduce Or Eliminate My Estate Taxes?

No. Only married persons can use a tax planning living trust.

What Happens To Assets That I Forget To Retitle To My Trust?

Assets not formally titled in your trust name are not protected and could be probated.

Do I Have To Appraise My Assets When I Transfer Them Into My Living Trust?

No.

Is The Living Trust Legal In All 50 States?

Yes.

Will I Lose Any Income Tax Deductions By Placing My Assets Into My Living Trust?

No.

Can I Make A Gift To Charity With My Living Trust?

Yes.

Do The Assets In My Living Trust Receive The "Step-Up In Basis" After My Death?

Yes.

Can I Use A Living Trust To Protect My Special Needs Child?

Yes. A "special needs trust" providing limited protection for the child can be included within your living trust. This prevents the child's share of your estate from being taken by a government agency, yet still allows the disabled child to receive any governmental benefits that he/she is entitled to. The child's trust fund is used only to *supplement* governmental benefits, not to replace them.

Can I Provide For My Pets In My Living Trust?

Yes. A living trust can include special provisions so that your pets will receive care after your death.

Can I Have More Than One Living Trust At The Same Time?

Yes. For example, a husband could set up his own trust for his separate assets. He and his wife could also set up a joint living trust to hold their marital assets.

Can I Change Or Revoke My Living Trust?

Yes.

Can My Living Trust Be Changed Or Revoked By My Back-up Trustees Or My Beneficiaries?

No. Only you as the creator/owner of your trust have the right to change or revoke it.

If I Replace My Old Will With A Living Trust Do I Have To Notify The Attorney Who Prepared It?

No. Even if your attorney kept a copy of your will there is no requirement that the attorney be notified. You should destroy all old wills you have in your possession (but only after you have signed your living trust!) to avoid any confusion.

Can One Living Trust Hold All Of My Assets, Including Those Located In Other States?

Yes.

How Do I Know My Back-Up Trustee Will Follow My Trust Instructions?

Back-up trustees have a strict legal duty (under trust law) to follow your trust instructions. If they don't, they can be replaced as trustee and held personally liable.

Is My Back-Up Trustee Personally Responsible To My Creditors?

No. A back-up trustee's personal assets are *not* subject to creditor claims against the trust.

Do My Back-Up Trustees Have To Live In The Same State That I Do?

No. A back-up trustee may live anywhere. Select your back-ups on the basis of trustworthiness, ability, and character, not geographical location.

Can I Have Co-Back-Up Trustees?

Yes.

How Old Does A Back-Up Trustee Have To Be?

Eighteen years is the minimum age in most states.

Is A Trustee Entitled To Be Paid?

Yes. A corporate trustee will charge a fee when it begins to act. Individual trustees are allowed *reasonable compensation* plus reimbursement for out-of-pocket expenses but, if you wish, you can direct that no compensation be paid or limit it to a specific amount.

Is The Cost Of Setting Up A Living Trust Tax Deductible?

No. The costs of the trust, durable power of attorney, pour-over will, etc., are *not* deductible items. However, costs specifically relating to estate tax planning such as the additional cost of the *estate tax planning provisions* may be tax deductible. They are reported as "miscellaneous deductions" on your income tax return. Check with your tax adviser and make certain your attorney allocates a portion of your bill to estate tax planning if you are setting up a tax planning trust.

Does A Living Trust Affect My Social Security Benefits?

No.

How Old Does A Person Have To Be To Set Up A Living Trust?

Eighteen years in most states.

Can I Still Deduct My Mortgage Interest If I Put My Home Into A Living Trust?

Yes.

If I Put My Rental Properties Into My Living Trust, How Are The Income And Expenses Treated?

The rental income and expenses (depreciation, for example) will be reported on your individual income tax returns just like before.

Can Two Single Persons Have A Joint Living Trust Like Married Couples Do?

Yes.

Will Setting Up A Living Trust Require Me To Open New Accounts?

No. Your existing accounts (checking, savings, brokerage, etc.) are retitled in your trust name. Be aware, however, that you may have to open a new account if you have already added other names on it.

Who Transfers The Assets Into My Living Trust?

Except for the quit claim deeds (which should be prepared by your attorney), you can easily transfer your assets into your trust yourself by following the instructions and forms your attorney should provide.

What Assets Should Be Put Into My Living Trust?

Everything. Any asset not correctly titled in your trust name is outside your trust estate plan and could be probated.

What About Registered Animals Such As Horses, Cattle, Etc.?

Have the certificate of registration reissued in the trust name, or assign the registration certificate to the trust. Your attorney should be able to provide you with the required assignment forms.

Should My Safe Deposit Box Be Rented In My Living Trust Name?

Yes.

Congress has no legal authority to take away living trusts

Single persons are especially vulnerable to probate

Should My Homeowner And Automobile Insurance Policies Be Put Into My Living Trust?

No. But for maximum protection it is a good idea to ask your insurance company to include your living trust on your policies as an *"additional insured."* This means that you are insured as an "individual" and also in your capacity as "trustee" of your trust. There should be no additional cost to do this.

Is An Attorney Needed To "Settle" My Living Trust When I Die?

No. Trust law gives your back-up trustee the legal authority to settle your trust. If you have a tax planning trust, then you may want to use a tax attorney or CPA to assist with dividing the assets and filing the appropriate estate tax returns following the death of each spouse—but this is an option, not a requirement.

Can Congress Take Away The Living Trust?

No. The United States Constitution reserves certain powers to the states, one of which is the right to create living trusts. Congress has no legal authority to take away living trusts.

Should I Have A Living Trust If I Am Single?

Absolutely. Single persons are especially vulnerable to probate.

How Much Can I Have Before I Am Subject To The Federal Estate Tax?

If your estate's *net* value (the value of all of your assets minus your debts) is *more* than $600,000 when you die, federal estate taxes must be paid from your estate. Remember, though, that this has nothing to do with probate costs, which can affect any size estate.

Do I Have To Register My Living Trust Document?

No. A few states may require you to file a short form certificate of trust to identify certain basic information about the trust such as its date, the names of the grantor, acting and back-up trustees, etc. However, the trust document itself is a private document and does not have to be registered or recorded anywhere.

Can A Living Trust Be Contested?

Yes. However, this is much more difficult than contesting a will. And your living trust can't be contested in probate court. The lawsuit must be filed in civil court. Unlike a will contest, the trustee retains control and may proceed with the distribution of the trust assets to the beneficiaries and may even terminate the trust (meaning that the lawsuit must then be expanded to include each beneficiary). It is very difficult to successfully contest a properly prepared living trust.

Can I Use A Living Trust To Disinherit My Children?

Yes.

My Spouse And I Have A Joint Living Trust. What Happens When One Of Us Dies?

Nothing. The surviving spouse is now the owner and acting trustee and has complete control of the trust. The trust document does not have to be changed.

Is It Difficult To Change My Living Trust?

No. Your trust can easily be amended. Most living trust attorneys charge a nominal fee for simple amendments, such as changing trustees, guardians, etc.

Do I Have To Pay Annual Maintenance Fees For My Living Trust?

No. But if you have named a corporate trustee, it will charge a fee when it begins acting as trustee.

What Happens To My Living Trust If I Marry or Remarry?

That depends on you. If you want to prevent your spouse or his/her family from acquiring any rights to your assets, then you will retain your trust to keep your separate assets *outside* the marriage. In this case, the living trust can make a very effective form of pre-nuptial agreement.

On the other hand, you may wish to include your spouse, which means your trust would be amended to add your spouse as a co-owner and co-trustee and to include his/her assets in the trust.

It is very difficult to successfully contest a properly prepared living trust

If I Get Divorced, What Happens To My Living Trust?

The divorce court will divide the marital property and debts between you and your spouse. One spouse will retain the living trust for his/her, now separate, property. The other spouse will revoke his/her interest in the trust, remove his/her assets from it, and will then need to set up a new living trust.

Do I Have To Put My Trust Name On My Checks?

No. We do recommend it though when you reorder your checks. This helps you become familiar with your trust name and serves as a reminder that all of your assets must be properly titled in the trust name to be protected.

Can I Put My Family Corporation Into My Living Trust?

Yes. Have your stock certificates re-issued in your trust name. Nothing else needs to be done. This includes stock in sub-chapter S "sub S" corporations and membership certificates in limited liability companies.

What About My Partnership Interests?

Your partnership interests are "assigned" to your trust. The other partners and the partnership assets are not affected.

What If I Own Real Estate In Shares With Another Person?

You quit claim *your share* of the real estate to your living trust. The other owner's share is not affected.

How Long Does It Take To Get A Living Trust?

In an emergency, it can be prepared in a day or two. Under normal circumstances, it should only take a few weeks to prepare the legal documents after you make the basic decisions. After signing your documents, allow a few more weeks to retitle your assets and beneficiary designations in the trust name.

Is It Hard To Transfer Assets Into My Living Trust?

No. It's easy. Your attorney should provide you with the necessary transfer letters and written instructions and allow you free telephone consultations and office visits if you have questions later on.

Have your stock certificates re-issued in your trust name

Can My Living Trust Leave All Or Part Of My Estate To An Unborn Child Or Grandchild?

Yes. Your trust can be set up to leave assets to an individual who has not yet been conceived. For example, it is quite common to leave a specific amount or percentage of your estate to your grandchildren. At the time you set up your trust you may have only one grandchild, but over the years you may eventually have many grandchildren. Your trust can be written so it automatically includes the additional grandchildren without having to change the trust document.

If My Child Dies Before Me, Does His/Her Spouse Inherit My Child's Share Of The Estate?

No. In-laws do not inherit directly from your estate unless you specifically provide for them. Most people want to distribute their assets to individuals who are related by blood or adoption, but rarely by marriage.

When Does My Living Trust End?

Once the assets are distributed to the beneficiaries the trust ends.

Who Keeps A Record Of The Assets In The Living Trust?

You do, and you don't have to tell your attorney or anyone else that you're buying and selling trust assets. Just make sure any assets you acquire are correctly titled in the trust name.

How Long Can My Living Trust Continue After My Death?

That's up to you. Most living trusts terminate as soon as the bills and taxes are paid, and the assets are distributed to the beneficiaries. Some last much longer. A trust created for *private purposes* (to benefit family members, etc.) can continue for approximately 100 years after you die. Trusts set up for *charitable purposes* (as defined by the IRS) can continue *indefinitely* after your death.

How Do I Handle The Cash I Receive From The Sale Of My Home, Which Is In My Living Trust?

Deposit your house sale proceeds into whatever savings account or investment you desire. Just make sure the account is titled in your trust name. Nothing has to be done to the trust document itself.

Wβ've introduced many terms that may be new to you, so we've put together this list as a handy reference. There are also some legal terms that we have purposely not used in this book because we wanted to keep it easy to understand. But since you will probably feel more comfortable dealing with an attorney if you know some of his/her "legalese," we have defined some of those terms here also.

AB Trust - See tax planning trust.

Administrator - Person named by the court to represent the estate when there is no will or the will did not name an executor (female may be called administratrix); also called a personal representative.

Back-up Trustee - Also called successor trustee; person or institution named in the trust agreement who can take over should the first trustee die, resign or become unable to act.

Basis - The original cost of an asset; may be adjusted by several factors such as cost of certain improvements to the property, depreciation, etc. The taxable gain on the sale of an asset is the net sales price less adjusted basis. When the owner of property dies the *basis* is "stepped-up" to the value at the date of death.

Beneficiaries - In a living trust, the persons and/or organizations who receive the trust property after the death of the trust grantor.

By-Pass Trust - See tax planning trust.

Codicil - A written change or amendment to a will.

Conservator - One who is legally responsible for the care and well being of another person; if appointed by a court, the conservator is under the court's supervision.

Conservatorship - A court controlled program for persons who have been declared incompetent because they are unable to manage their own affairs. Also called a probate guardianship in some states.

Corporate Trustee - A bank, trust company or institution which is legally authorized to manage trusts.

Credit Shelter Trust - See tax planning trust.

Durable Power Of Attorney - See Power of Attorney.

Durable Power Of Attorney For Health Care - A special power of attorney that gives someone else the legal authority to make health care decisions for you in the event you are unable to make them for yourself; also called a Health Care Directive.

Estate - Property and debts left by an individual at death.

Estate Taxes - Federal or state taxes on the value of the property left at death; often called inheritance tax or death tax.

Executor - Person or institution named in a will to carry out its instructions (female is executrix); also called a personal representative.

Fiduciary - Person having the legal duty to act for another's benefit; implies great confidence and trust, and a high degree of good faith; (usually associated with a trustee).

Gain - When property is sold, the difference between what you receive and what you paid for it; used to determine the amount of taxes owed.

Grantor - The person who sets up or creates the trust; also called the trustor, settlor or creator.

Grantor Trust - The name the IRS uses for a revocable living trust.

Gross Estate - The value of an estate without deduction for debts, mortgages, etc. Probate fees are usually calculated on the gross value of the estate.

Guardian - One who is legally responsible for the care and well-being of another person who is either incapacitated or a minor; appointed by the court and under the court's supervision.

Guardian of the Estate - One who is appointed to manage the assets of a minor. (See also conservator.)

Health Care Directive - See Durable Power of Attorney for Health Care.

Holographic Will - A handwritten will.

Incapacitated/Incompetent - One who is unable to manage his/her own affairs, either temporarily or permanently; also applies to minor children; lack of legal power.

Intestate - Without a will.

Irrevocable Trust - Opposite of revocable trust; a trust that cannot be changed (revoked) or cancelled once it is set up.

Joint Ownership - Also called joint ownership with right of survivorship or joint tenancy; when two or more persons own the same property; death of a joint owner immediately transfers ownership to the surviving joint owners; different from tenancy-in-common (see below).

Living Trust - A written legal document into which you place all of your property, with instructions for its management and distribution upon your incapacity or death; also known as a revocable inter vivos trust; a trust created during one's lifetime.

Living Will - A written document stating that you do not wish to be kept alive by artificial means when the illness or injury is terminal or when you are irreversibly vegetative or "brain dead."

Marital Deduction - The amount you may give your spouse free of gift or estate taxes; this amount is currently unlimited.

Minor Child - A child under the legal age for an adult; varies by state (usually under 18).

Net Value - The value of an estate after deducting debts, mortgages, etc. Federal estate taxes are based on the net value of an estate.

Per Capita - A way of distributing your estate so all members of the group take equally; share and share alike; if a member of the group is deceased, the estate is shared equally by the surviving members (not to the descendants of the deceased person); opposite of per stirpes.

Per Stirpes - A way of distributing your estate by right of representation. If you leave your estate to your children, per stirpes, a deceased child's share will go to his or her child(ren) in equal shares; also called by right of representation; opposite of per capita.

Personal Property - Movable property (as opposed to real property which is permanent, such as land); includes furniture, automobiles, equipment, cash and stocks.

Personal Representative - Another name for an executor or administrator.

Power of Attorney - A legal document giving another person legal authority to sign your name on your behalf in your absence (different from the fiduciary duty of a trustee); ends at incapacity or death; some states permit a durable power of attorney which is valid through incapacity and ends at death. These are general powers of attorney. There are also limited powers of attorney which give someone only limited authority for a very specific purpose (for example, to transfer a car title).

Probate - *With a will (see testate)*—the legal process of filing a will with the probate court; the court determines if the will is valid, hears all claims, orders creditors paid and property distributed according to the terms of the will.

Without a will (see intestate)—the legal process of the probate court receiving all claims, ordering creditors paid and property distributed according to the laws of that state (the state's will).

Probate Guardianship - A court controlled program to manage the affairs of minor children or incapacitated persons. In some states, also called a *conservatorship*.

QTIP Trust - See Tax planning trust.

Real Property - Land and property which is "permanently" attached to land (such as a house).

Revocable Trust - Opposite of irrevocable trust; a trust in which the person setting it up retains the power to change (revoke) or cancel the trust during his/her lifetime.

Simple Pour Over Will - A short will used with a living trust; states that any property left out of your living trust will "pour over" into your living trust upon your death.

Special Gifts - A separate listing of special property to go to selected persons; also called special bequests.

Spouse - Husband or wife.

Step-Up In Basis - See basis.

Tax Planning Trust - Living trust with special provisions to reduce or eliminate federal estate taxes; can only be used by married persons.

Tenancy-In-Common - A form of joint ownership in which two or more persons own the same property in shares; at death of a tenant-in-common, ownership transfers to that person's heirs, not to the other owner; different from joint ownership/joint tenancy (see above).

Testamentary Trust - A trust set up in a will that only takes effect after death.

Testate - One who dies with a will.

Transfer on Death Designation (TOD) - Naming a beneficiary on an asset; when the owner dies the beneficiary immediately owns the property without probate; also called pay on death, TOD or POD.

Trustee - Person or institution agreeing to accept and manage property according to the provisions of the trust agreement.

Will - A written document with instructions for disposing of property at death; can only be enforced through the probate court.

LIVING TRUST INFORMATION FORM

Date_____/_____/_____

Instructions: Print or type. Write **n/a** if an item does not apply. Use estimated amounts and attach additional sheets if you need more space.

1. PERSONAL INFORMATION

Your Marital Status: Single❏ Married❏ Divorced❏ Widowed❏   County of Residence_____

Your Name (first, middle, last)   Date of Birth

1 2 3 4 5 6 7 8   9 10 11 12   13 14 15 16   17 18 19 20

Grade School   *High School*   *College*   *Graduate School*

Your Education (circle highest number of years completed)

Your Spouse's Name (first, middle, last)   Date of Birth

1 2 3 4 5 6 7 8   9 10 11 12   13 14 15 16   17 18 19 20

Grade School   *High School*   *College*   *Graduate School*

Your Spouse's Education (circle highest number of years completed)

Home Address (number, street)	City	State	Zip Plus 4 Digit

Mailing Address (number, street) *(if different from home)*	City	State	Zip Plus 4 digit

(   )   (   )   (   )

Home Phone   Work Phone   Spouse's Work Phone

Your Employer's Name   Your Occupation

Your Spouse's Employer's Name   Spouse's Occupation

GENERAL INFORMATION

Yes   No   Do you have a family attorney?

Yes   No   Have you ever used an attorney before?

Yes   No   Are you a United States citizen?

Yes   No   Is your spouse a United States citizen?

Yes   No   Do you have a will or living trust now?   } If yes, attach copy to this form.

Yes   No   Does your spouse have a will or living trust now?

Yes   No   Do you have a burial lot?_____

              In What Name   Cemetery   City   State

Yes   No   Are you or your spouse expecting to receive property or money from:

          Inheritance/Judgment/Gift/Lawsuit/Other? If yes, approximately how much?_____

Yes   No   Are you or your spouse custodian of property under the Uniform Gifts to Minors

          Act? If yes, what is the approximate value?_____

          How many living children do you have?_____Your Spouse?_____

          How many deceased children do you have?_____Your Spouse?_____

Yes No   Are all of your children natural or legally adopted?

Yes No   Are there any stepchildren in your family? If yes, how many?

Yes No   Do you have any children or other dependents with special needs?

If yes describe the needs:_____

How many children under age 18 do you have?_____

How many grandchildren do you have?_____ How many under age 18?_____

Your <u>father/mother</u> is still living. Your spouse's <u>father/mother</u> is still living.
    circle   circle

You have_____ living and _____ deceased brothers and sisters.

Your spouse has _____ living and _____deceased brothers and sisters.

You have _____ step-brothers and step-sisters.

Your spouse has_____ step-brothers and step-sisters.

2. FINANCIAL INFORMATION

A.   Yes   No   Do you own a **home** or any other **real estate**?
Attach a copy of all your current deeds.

Property (Address)	Titled In Whose Name	Market Value (-)	Mortgage (=)	Equity
			Total Net Value	$

B.   Yes   No   Do you own any **other titled property**? (Car, boat, etc.)?

Describe Property	Titled In Whose Name	Market Value (-)	Loan (=)	Equity
			Total Net Value	$

C.   Yes   No   Do you have any **checking accounts**?

Name Of Bank	Titled In Whose Name	Approx. Balance
	Total Value	$

Detach Here

LIVING TRUST INFORMATION FORM

Detach Here

D. Yes No Do you have any **savings accounts, CDs, or money market accounts**?

Name Of Bank	Titled In Whose Name	Appox. Balance
	Total Value	$

E. Yes No Do you own any **stocks, bonds, or mutual funds**?

Name Of Security	Titled In Whose Name	Value
	Total Value	$

F. Yes No Do you have any **tax deferred savings** (IRA, 401(k), Keoghs, qualified annuities, pension/profit sharing)?

Description	Owner	Beneficiary	Age	Value
		Total Value		$

G. Yes No Do you have any **insurance policies**?

Name Of Company	Owner	Beneficiary	Age	Death Benefit
		Total Value		$

H. Yes No Do you have any **valuable items** (Coin collections, antiques, jewelry, art, heirlooms, etc.)? If yes, list below or on a separate sheet.

General Description	Approx. Value
Total Value	$

Living Trust Information Form

I. Yes   No   Does anyone **owe you money** (Loans to children, contracts for deed, etc.)? If yes, attach copy of your paperwork.

General Description	Who owes you?	Approx. Balance Owed
	Total Value	$

J. Estimate the approximate value of all your remaining **personal property** that has not been listed above. (Personal effects: clothes, appliances, furniture, etc.) $ _____

K. Yes   No   Do you have any **debts** (Other than your mortgages and loans listed above) such as credit cards, personal loans, etc?

Who Do You Owe?	Amount Owed
Total Debt	$

L. Yes   No   Have you **co-signed or guaranteed any loans**?

Description Of Loan	Co-signed For Whom	Amount Owed
	Total Debt	$

M. **Total value** of everything you and your spouse **own**.
(add line A thru J above) $ _____

N. **Total value** of everything you and your spouse **owe**.
(add line K and line L above) $ _____

O. Subtract line **N** from line **M**.   TOTAL ESTATE NET VALUE = $ _____

P. Yes   No   Do you have a safe deposit box?

Name Of Bank	Rented In Whose Name

Detach Here

A. **My Trustees:** Controls and manages your trust - usually you and your spouse.

Name _____

Name _____

B. **My Back-up Trustees:** Takes over at your incapacity or death - usually adult children or trusted relative or friend.

#1 Choice: _____

Name   City   State

#2 Choice: _____

Name   City   State

#3 Choice:_____

Name   City   State

C. **Guardians For My Minor Children:** Raises your children if you become incapacitated or die.

#1 Choice: _____

Name   City   State

#2 Choice: _____

Name   City   State

#3 Choice:_____

Name   City   State

D. **Trustees For My Minor Children:** Manages your children's inheritance. Can be the same person as their guardian.

#1 Choice: _____

Name   City   State

#2 Choice: _____

Name   City   State

#3 Choice:_____

Name   City   State

E. **My Health Care Agent:** Authorized to make medical decisions if you are unable. Can be different persons than your trustees.

#1 Choice: _____

Name   City   State

#2 Choice: _____

Name   City   State

#3 Choice:_____

Name   City   State

F. Yes   No   Do you or your spouse want to sign a **living will**?

Detach Here

LIVING TRUST INFORMATION FORM

G. Beneficiaries

Special Gifts - Organizations: Do you want to make a gift (Cash or specific item) to a charity, school, or religious organization?

Name Of Organization	Description Of Gift

Special Gifts - Individuals: Do you want to give any specific items to a family member or other individual?

Name Of Person	Description Of Gift

Your Beneficiaries: Who do you want to receive the rest of your estate after the special gifts have been distributed?

Name Of Person	Percentage/Amount	Age

Detach Here

H. **Age Of Distribution:** Do you want your children to receive their inheritance all at one time, or in installments at certain ages? Explain below.

I. **Dependents With Special Needs:** Do you want provisions included in your trust to protect a special needs dependent? Explain Below.

J. **Disinheriting**: Is there any person you want to exclude from your estate?

Name Of Person	Relationship To You

K. **Alternative Beneficiaries:** Who do you want to receive your estate if you and your spouse outlive all of the beneficiaries you've listed above?

Name Of Person/Organization	Percentage/Amount

L. **Special Trust Instructions:** Do you have any special instructions (other than those listed above) you want included in your trust. Briefly explain below.

LIVING TRUST INFORMATION FORM

LIST ANY QUESTIONS THAT YOU WANT TO DISCUSS WITH YOUR ATTORNEY HERE.

Detach Here

Copyright ©1995 by Hudspeth Publishing Company
5904 East Bannister Road, Kansas City, Missouri 64134-1141 • (816) 765-3900

Detach Here

DON'T WAIT! AVOID PROBATE!

SPECIAL SAVINGS BOOK ORDER FORM

Share the peace of mind, financial protection, tax savings and additional benefits of a living trust estate plan with your loved ones and friends. To purchase additional copies of *The Living Trust Alternative*, you can:

1.   Check with your local bookstore. They will order additional copies for you if they are sold out.

2.   Or, you can order directly from us by using the order form below.

The Living Trust Alternative is also available on audio cassette. This dynamic program will take you to an actual public seminar featuring Louis Austin, living trust attorney, who is known to many as the "voice of living trust." As he explains the revocable living trust in conversational language, you will understand how living trust estate planning benefits everyone. This interesting and important information closely parallels and expands upon his book.

The audio cassette also includes a live radio interview. Louis Austin discusses the most commonly asked questions about living trusts. This set of two cassettes can be ordered for $9.95. Order now! Only a limited number of cassettes are still available.

SPECIAL BONUS

Buy 2 books for $37.90 (plus shipping and handling),
receive the audio cassette tape set **Absolutely Free**. Save $9.95!

SPECIAL SAVINGS BOOK ORDER FORM

Please print or type.

Ship To:

Name:_____

_____

_____

Number:_____ Street:_____

City State Zip:_____

Telephone:_____
(We may have questions about your order.)

Method of payment:

❑ Mastercard/VISA   ❑ Check enclosed

Acct. # _____

Expiration Date:_____

Signature:_____

Name Printed: _____

Telephone: (___)_____
(If different from above.)

Item	Quantity	Price	Shipping/Handling	Total Cost
Book	1	$18.95	$4.00	$22.95
Cassette	1	$ 9.95	$3.00	$12.95
Special Bonus 2 Books & Cassette		$37.90	$5.00	$42.90
MO residents add 6.47% sales tax				$
TOTAL PAYMENT ENCLOSED				$

Δ QUICK SHIP. Call 816-765-3900
    (M.-F., 9 a.m.- 5 p.m. Central Time)

Δ INSTANT ORDERS BY FAX!
    816-765-1689

Δ Quantity discounts are available on larger orders.
    Call or write for details.

Mail To: Hudspeth Publishing Company
5904 East Bannister Road, Kansas City, Missouri 64134-1141 • **(816) 765-3900** • Allow 2 -3 weeks for delivery.

AUS 064.3 (6/95)